CAPITALISM AND THE WELFARE STATE

CAPITALISM AND THE WELFARE STATE

DILEMMAS OF SOCIAL BENEVOLENCE

NEIL GILBERT

YALE UNIVERSITY PRESS
NEW HAVEN AND LONDON

To Barbara, Evan, and Jesse

Designed by Nancy Ovedovitz and set in ITC Garamond type by
Ro-Mark Typographic Co., Inc. Printed in the United States of America by
Edwards Brothers Inc., Ann Arbor, Michigan.

Library of Congress Cataloging in Publication Data

Gilbert, Neil.
  Capitalism and the welfare state.
  Includes index.
  1. Social services—United States. 2. United States—
Social policy. 3. Welfare state. 4. United States—
Economic conditions—1961-   . 5. Capitalism.
I. Title.
HV95.G5   1983   361'.973   83-42872
ISBN 0-300-03112-2

          3   5   7   9   10   8   6   4   2

CONTENTS

PREFACE

This book is about the American welfare state as it has evolved in a capitalist economy over the last two decades. During that time the welfare state experienced a difficult and unexpected turn of events, as it went from an era of public approval and expansion under the Great Society programs of the 1960s to a period of disfavor and retrenchment in the early 1980s.

The mid-1960s was an exciting time for social welfare planners and policymakers. A vast array of new social welfare programs was unfolding under the Economic Opportunity Act of 1964, the Demonstration Cities and Metropolitan Development Act of 1966, the Older Americans Act of 1965, the Food Stamp Act of 1964, the Community Mental Health Centers Act of 1963, Medicare and Medicaid in 1965, and other legislative initiatives of the Great Society. New political constituencies were forged in support of these programs. The excitement of planning these activities was enhanced by the generous supply of public funds made available to implement them. Between 1960 and 1976 public expenditures for social welfare grew from 10.5 to 20.4% of the gross national product; in dollars this represented an increase from approximately $50 billion to more than $300 billion. Social welfare planners could hardly keep pace with the demands for innovative program ideas and the development of structures to implement them as rapidly as possible. With attention focused on opportunities for program expansion and the quick course of events, it was difficult to gain a comprehensive view of the welfare state and the directions in which it was headed. Faced with the immediate challenge of designing programs to solve America's social problems, planners and policymakers had little time or inclination to confront in a rational way the larger issues of managing the growth and development of a welfare state in a capitalist society. The failure to give these issues sufficient attention has left the welfare state vulnerable to the siege visited upon it in the early 1980s.

My analytic perspective on the predicaments of a welfare state in a capitalist society is influenced by at least three assumptions that should be made explicit to the reader. First, the contemporary system of American capitalism, broadly understood to involve a mixture of both private enterprise and elements of governmental control, is for the foreseeable future the pervasive arrangement under which production and consumption will be organized in American society. While some may believe that other arrangements—from abolishing private enterprise to eliminating government regulation—would be more desirable, I begin my analysis from the standpoint of what exists and presumably will continue in an American democracy. From this perspective, one's views on change lean toward adjustments and modifications rather than fundamental restructuring of a social system. Second, while the welfare state performs many functions, including social control, its progressive and benevolent objectives reflect the predominant motives underlying its development in modern times. Finally, although there are tensions inherent in the relationship between the social market of the welfare state and the economic market of the capitalist system, with careful management and a sense of proportion this relationship may be reconciled to the benefit of the commonweal. This last assumption draws attention to what is perhaps the most central structural problem with which architects of the welfare state must come to grips: the task of creating a workable balance between the welfare state and the market economy.

In grappling with this problem it is useful to understand the nature and boundaries of the social market as it has evolved in recent years. With that objective in mind, the first three sections of this book examine various facets of the changing relationship between the welfare state and the market economy. In part I, "The Merging of Economic and Social Markets," I analyze a series of developments in the welfare state, such as the influx of profit-making organizations and schemes to stimulate competition among providers of social services. These developments are drawn together to illustrate the converging lines of a trend toward the commercialization of the social market.

Some of the underlying reasons for that trend are considered in part II, "The Plight of Universal Social Services." Here the analysis focuses upon the expanded scope and purpose of social services, and increases in entitlements granted to the middle class since the 1960s. The implications of these changes are appraised in light of their impact on the boundaries between the social and economic markets.

In part III, "Voluntary Alternatives," I examine critically the growing emphasis on the provision of aid through the voluntary sector of the social market. Social supports that can be provided by informal networks of family and friends are considered along with the possibilities for aid that can be expected from formal voluntary agencies. An analysis of current trends in family life, for example, suggests that there has been a substantial shift in the investment of labor from the home to the market economy. In the realm of family policy this trend has led to considerable need and much support for provisions such as day care for children and flextime in work schedules to accommodate the problems of working mothers. Yet to achieve greater balance in this realm and to strengthen the resiliency of voluntary aid, there seems also to be a need for alternative policies designed to encourage the provision of more informal family care, especially during the early years of child rearing.

The concluding section, part IV, "The Future of Welfare Capitalism," begins with an effort to synthesize the main features of the American welfare state as they have evolved over the last two decades. Turning to the future, I explore a course for strengthening the welfare state's position in a mixed economy as we approach the end of the twentieth century. This course requires formulating a clear vision of the scope, structure, methods, and distinctive purposes of the social market. My intent in exploring these elements of the social market is not to discover the equation for a workable balance between social welfare and capitalism but to frame the issues for debate and to excite the spirit of inquiry.

ACKNOWLEDGMENTS

My work on this book has benefited from the generous assistance of a number of people. I am particularly grateful to my good friend and colleague Harry Specht, who read the entire manuscript and prepared a detailed critique that was enormously helpful. I am also indebted to James Torczyner and Adam Graycar for their thoughtful suggestions.

During the final draft of this book I presented most of the manuscript in a doctoral seminar to a group of Berkeley students whose critical faculties were not at all inhibited by the author's presence and academic authority. For their frank and intellectually stimulating observations I should like to thank Erica Baum, David Lindeman, Amanda Smith, Maria Talbott, and Angela Browne, who also gave unstintingly of her time and effort as my research assistant.

I was fortunate to receive a Fulbright Fellowship in 1981 that provided an opportunity to compare American trends in social welfare to recent experiences in the British welfare state, several examples of which are included in this book. My good fortune in this instance was magnified through association with David Jones, David Thomas, Ken Judge, Howard Glennerster, and other British colleagues whose information and congenial advice were most instructive. Additional financial assistance for this study was received from the Committee on Research at the University of California, Berkeley.

I am obliged to the editors of *Society, Social Service Review, Social Work,* and the *Journal of Policy Analysis and Management* for permission to incorporate in this book revised portions of articles that have appeared in these journals.*

The kind support of Gladys Topkis at Yale University Press greatly enhanced the process of bringing this book to publication. Through-

*Neil Gilbert, "The Future of Welfare Capitalism," *Society,* 18: 6 (1981); "The Plight of Universal Social Services," *Journal of Policy Analysis and Management,* 1: 3 (Spring 1982); "The Transformation of Social Services," *Social Service Review,* 51: 4 (Dec. 1977); "Policy Issues in Primary Prevention," *Social Work,* 27: 4 (July 1982); and "In Support of Domesticity," *Journal of Policy Analysis and Management,* 2: 4 (Summer 1983).

out that process my family was an unfailing source of inspiration, warmth, and good cheer.

PART I

THE MERGING OF ECONOMIC AND SOCIAL MARKETS

ONE

WELFARE FOR PROFIT

At the turn of the twentieth century *welfare capitalism* was an idea gaining favor among American businessmen. In practice, this notion involved industry's attending to the social needs of workers through an assortment of medical and funeral benefits, as well as provisions for recreational, educational, housing, and social services. These early welfare measures were embraced with mixed motives. In extending their concern for the conditions of employee life beyond the production line, business leaders were certainly influenced by their need to mold a disciplined industrial work force out of the immigrant masses—an unpredictable, sometimes dangerous lot. It was also believed that the provision of welfare benefits under industrial auspices strengthened the bond between worker and company, which diminished gravitation toward trade unions. The rise of welfare capitalism was fueled as much by these self-interests as by any altruistic desires to ameliorate the conditions of working people. In whatever proportion these different motives influenced specific cases, the overall appeal of welfare capitalism to industrial leaders might be summed up in the thought that through these arrangements "business could do well by doing good."

How much good was actually done under the early system of welfare capitalism is debated among historians of industrial relations, a debate often clouded by pro-business and pro-unionist sentiments. Standing clear of partisan positions, Stuart Brandes's analysis weighs the virtues and deficiencies of welfare capitalism with an even hand. On the balance, he suggests that these arrangements provided an expedient solution to problems of industrialization that was minimally acceptable but left much to be desired.[1] It was better than nothing, which was the other main alternative during much of the brief, but turbulent, period that welfare capitalism flourished.

By the mid-1920s, welfare capitalism had reached the apex of its popularity among business leaders. The gradual rise of this early blend of capitalism and welfare occurred over a period of roughly fifty

3

years; its decline followed the stock market crash of 1929 and was as precipitous. As the Great Depression deepened, welfare provisions were generally the first items to be jettisoned by industry. While the depression contributed measurably to the undoing of welfare capital-ism, there are reasons to believe that it merely hastened the inevita-ble. The system was not universally preferred; employees often re-sented its paternalistic character; labor leaders, of course, were adamant in their opposition; and some employers viewed it as mol-lycoddling workers. Furthermore, as Brandes points out, if provisions of housing, recreation, education, social work, and other welfare programs had remained business functions much beyond the 1930s, the growing complexity and expense of their administration surely would have led business to reconsider the benefits of this system.[2] With the depression and the coming of the New Deal, business was spared the need to decide the utility of creating large welfare bu-reaucracies in the midst of industrial organizations.

The New Deal transformed the relationship between welfare and capitalism. As responsibility for many welfare functions passed from the hands of business and local communities to the federal bureauc-racies, the foundation of the modern welfare state took shape. It was rapidly built upon. Between 1929 and 1975 the size and scope of welfare bureaucracies under government aegis multiplied, as re-flected in constant dollar expenditures, from a $12- to $286-billion enterprise. Under government consolidation, welfare programs that were once an industrial appendage have become a separate and powerful force in capitalist society. With this development the idea of *welfare capitalism* entered a second phase.

In the early 1950s Richard Crossman wrote about the relationship between welfare and capitalism, describing the manner in which the British welfare state had "civilised" capitalism.[3] In the sense that Crossman used the term, *welfare capitalism* expressed a symbiotic relationship between a social and an economic market that represent two dissimilar modes for the production and distribution of benefits in society. It is a relationship that bonds individual ambitions and collective responsibility. Capitalism encourages competition and risk-taking behavior. Although success in the economic marketplace is often well rewarded, misfortune and failure can lead to harsh consequences. There are few market mechanisms to mitigate the consequences of accident, illness, age, and vicissitudes of industrial society. And these mechanisms, such as private insurance, provide the most protection to those who are relatively well off and least in need of it. The welfare state operates through a social market that provides a sort of communal safety net for the casualties of a market economy. Ideally, as a system for distributing benefits in society, the market economy responds to individual initiative, ability, productivity, and the desire for profit. In contrast, the social market of the welfare state responds to need, dependency, and charitable impulses. Although need and ability to pay strongly influence the allocation of provisions in social and economic markets, these systems of exchange are not exempt from political forces. As Pinker notes, despite need or ability to pay, some individuals receive more or less provision because of the extent to which they meet ideological, religious, or ethnic criteria of political desert.[4]

The symbiotic relationship of welfare capitalism is not without customary tensions and contradictions. Indeed, one might say that these tensions maintain a social balance between regard for charity and profit (or need and merit) that contributes to a healthy capitalist society.[5] (Of course, some people may deny the initial premise that a capitalist society can be healthy in any form, and for them much analysis in this book will seem critically flawed.) However, this balance is tenuous and once again seems to be shifting in a new direction. With the social market undergoing pressure to adopt the values and methods of the economic market, a third phase of welfare capitalism is on the horizon.

PUBLIC AND PRIVATE WELFARE

While the British welfare state is more inclusive than its American counterpart, the difference today is more a matter of degree than kind. Crossman's interpretation of the relationship between welfare and capitalism that characterized the British system in 1952 also describes the system that had evolved in the United States by the late 1960s. However, between 1970 and 1980 a series of developments in the American welfare state forecast a new meaning for the term *welfare capitalism*, which fits neither the modern interpretations suggested by British socialists, such as Crossman, nor the early forms built on industrial welfare.[6] Though it has yet to be made explicit, the new meaning of *welfare capitalism* is based on an emerging view of the welfare state as an untapped market (with profit-making potential) which is ready for conversion to capitalist doctrine. This commercialization of the social market threatens to upset the symbiotic relationship between welfare and capitalist values. While it may not be possible to reconcile entirely the contradictions between welfare and capitalism, the insinuation of the profit motive and other aspects of this emergent phase of welfare capitalism raise some intriguing questions about the basic nature of the American welfare state and its future. Before exploring these questions let us briefly review how the welfare state has arrived at this juncture.

Up through the early 1960s the public and private sectors of the social welfare system in the United States were clearly distinguishable. In the public sector, social welfare services were financed by tax monies and delivered by agencies of local, state, and federal government. Funds for services in the private sector came from charitable bequests and other voluntary contributions. Services were delivered by private nonprofit agencies, often under the auspices of religious groups and ethnic associations. Owing little for support to the public sector, private agencies could march to a different beat. Traditionally, they were seen as the innovative sector of social welfare, where new ideas could be tried unencumbered by the rules, political constraints, and general plodding of public bureaucracies. The private sector also provided an arena for the expression of particularistic and sectarian values.

While there were incidents of public funding of private welfare services going as far back as 1819, when federal support was provided to the Hartford Asylum for the Deaf and Dumb, they were by and large intermittent events that did not take on the character of large-scale systematic efforts until recent times. Between 1930 and the mid-1960s the private sector of social welfare was relatively separate from government. Yet it was not "private" in the sense of being part of the market economy. Indeed, the private sector of social welfare is frequently referred to as the "voluntary sector," reflecting the absence of a profit motive and the philanthropic sources of its revenues. It consists of the "moral associations" that so impressed de Tocqueville in his studies of American life.[7] These are eleemosynary agencies concerned with furthering community well-being rather than creating financial gain.

In recent years there has been a substantial increase in government financing of social welfare activities. Between 1950 and 1965 public expenditures were fairly stable, moving from an estimated 65.9 to 64.3% of all spending for social welfare purposes. The slight drop was sharply reversed between 1965 and 1975. Over that period government outlays rose to cover an estimated 72.7% of all social welfare expenditures, which by 1975 totaled approximately $388.7 billion.[8] This growth in public financing was accompanied by two significant changes in the nature of the welfare state.

First, over the last decade the distinction between financing of services through the public and the private sectors of social welfare has faded close to the disappearing point. This transformation came about through the use of "purchase-of-service" arrangements, whereby public agencies contract with the private sector to provide social welfare services.[9] Opportunities for purchase of services from private agencies were generally limited through the early 1960s. Under the 1962 amendments to the Social Security Act, for example, public agencies were enjoined from using federal funds to purchase services in the private sector. These strictures upon purchase of service were loosened under the 1967 Social Security amendments, which authorized purchase arrangements for a wide array of activities. Between 1962 and 1973 there was an enormous expansion in the use of public funds to purchase services delivered by private agencies. During that period, for example, a study of the trend in government payments to Jewish-sponsored agencies reveals a twenty-fold increase in these payments from $27 million to $561 million. Thus in the brief span of one decade government payments as a proportion of the total income received by Jewish-sponsored agencies rose from 11 to 51%.[10]

However, one small hitch remained in financing the local matching share for purchase-of-service arrangements. That is, although the 1967 amendments allowed state agencies to purchase services directly from private agencies, private agency donations were not permitted to qualify for the states' 25% matching share of federal social service grants *if* these contributions reverted to the donor's facility. There were ways to circumvent this restriction. In practice it was not uncommon for a donation to be made by a United Fund organization with a request that their contribution be used to support a particular type of activity in a specified community, an activity performed by only one agency in that community—that agency being an affiliate of the United Fund organization.[11] In this fashion private donations could be implicitly earmarked as the local share for a designated agency.

In 1974 the Title XX amendments to the Social Security Act introduced a basic change in policy for financing the states' 25% local matching share of social service grants. Under Title XX, private agency donations are permitted to qualify for the local matching share even when they are used to purchase services from the donating agency, leaving an open field for public funds to finance private social service operations. By 1980 federal programs provided over 50% of all the financial support that went to private nonprofit social service and community development organizations.[12]

It all happened so quickly that those who make a habit of studying social welfare are still not sure of the implications this intermingling of public and private voluntary auspices holds for the future of the welfare state. Purchase of service has become a popular subject of investigation; grants are awarded and conferences are held to study its mechanics and implications. From the private sector the concern, of course, is that government encroachment upon agency autonomy lurks between the lines of the purchase-of-service contract. While the evidence on this matter is far from conclusive, Kramer's major cross-national study as well as other more limited investigations to date are consistent in suggesting that the acceptance of public financing has impinged little upon the autonomy of private social welfare agencies.[13] These agencies, Kramer reports, complained more about infringement on their autonomy by the United Way than about the low level of accountability demanded by government. This is an important point to bear in mind in examining the second change in the nature of the welfare state.

During the same period that purchase of service has made such a visible, if uncertain, impact, it has been quietly accompanied by a parallel development which in the long run may prove a more potent influence on the evolution of the welfare state. That development is the influx of profit-making organizations into the private sector of social welfare. Once an almost exclusive preserve of voluntary nonprofit organizations (moral associations dedicated to service), since the mid 1960s the private sector of social welfare has been penetrated by an increasing number of proprietary agencies dedicated to service at a profit.

Proprietary agencies are prominently represented in many social service program areas including: homemaker/chore, day care, transportation, meals-on-wheels, and employment training. The most conspicuous area is that of nursing home care. Between 1960 and 1970 the number of nursing home facilities increased by 140% and the number of beds tripled. Close to 80% of these facilities are operated for profit; public funds, mainly from the Medicaid Act of 1965, account for $2 out of every $3 in nursing home revenue.[14] This area of service is typically referred to as the nursing home "industry"; the child-care "industry" looms just over the horizon.[15]

Currently there are no figures on the overall scope of publicly funded social welfare provisions delivered through profit-oriented agencies. While it is estimated that in 1976 between 50 and 66% of the $2.5 billion spent on social services under Title XX of the Social Security Act involved purchase-of-service arrangements, it is almost impossible to determine how much of these funds went to profit-making agencies among the service providers.[16] This lack of knowledge derives partly from the fact that federal officials responsible for Title XX expenditures have not deemed the distinction between private nonprofit and proprietary agencies important enough to separate private purchase of services into these categories.

Even if this information were in demand, however, it would be extraordinarily difficult and costly to track purchase of services through the layers of governmental and private agencies, from state purchasers to local providers. Purchase-of-service arrangements often involve three or four parties. For example, a state Department of Public Welfare might use Title XX funds to purchase transportation services for the elderly from a State Unit on Aging, which in turn could distribute these funds to a dozen Area Agencies on Aging in the counties, and they might use the funds to purchase the actual services from local providers. In this example, the original purchase recorded on federal reporting forms is with a public agency, whereas the funds finally devolve to local providers, which may include public, private nonprofit, and private profit-making agencies. Multiply this example twenty times or so and one gets an idea of the work entailed for state agencies to monitor exactly what is being purchased from whom under purchase-of-service agreements in the Title XX program alone. Few state agencies have the technical capacity to undertake this effort.

The problem of gathering information on purchase of services reflects the basic predicament of maintaining a firm line of accountability between federal/state purchasers and private/local providers. The size and complexity of public/private purchase-of-service networks often result in fragmented and attenuated lines of accountability. This difficulty in achieving accountability may explain, in part, why public financing of the private social welfare sector has had little impact on the autonomy of private agencies. In any case the limited extent to which it is practicable to hold private social welfare agencies accountable to the public sector is an issue that gains force when we compare public financing of private nonprofit agencies with public financing of profit-making agencies.

FOR AND AGAINST PROFIT IN THE SOCIAL MARKET

Advocates of the welfare state are inclined to argue that the caring and aiding objectives of social welfare programs are better served by public and private nonprofit agencies than by profit-making organizations. Various justifications for this view are put forth on moral, empirical, and theoretical grounds. The moral argument is that it is simply wrong to profit from programs that meet poor people's needs for vital services. This is a curious proposition in a capitalist society where, after all, human needs for food, clothing, shelter, medicine, and other necessities of life are normally satisfied through profit-oriented transactions in the market economy. Yet there is something about profiting from the delivery of social welfare services that offends public sensibilities.

There are two explanations which suggest that public distaste for profit making in the realm of social welfare may stem more from psychological and economic concerns than ethical principles regarding the allocation of vital services. Social welfare services that tend to the needs of children, the elderly, and the disabled are activities traditionally performed by the family and inspired by love and the sense of personal commitment that bonds family life. The psychological explanation speculates that the public conscience is disturbed more by the intrusion of pecuniary motives into spheres of service traditionally associated with family duty than by the deed of profiting from vital services, which occurs regularly in the market economy.[17] *Tender Loving Greed*, the title of a study of abuses in the nursing home industry, is an evocative expression of the antipathy toward having the functions of family care assumed by agencies committed to economic gain. However, it must be said that this study found the quality of care at nonprofit homes was not necessarily better than that offered by proprietary homes.[18]

The economic explanation suggests that what is unseemly about profiting from social welfare services is neither the vital importance of these activities nor their association with the nurturing warmth of family life. According to Hansmann, profit making in the social services is viewed as improper mainly because competitive markets do not work well with these types of services.[19] From this perspective, expressions of public discomfort reflect more of a rational assessment that profit-making agencies will be ineffective and inefficient in the social market than of a moral judgment about the decency of this arrangement. If profit-oriented agencies offered the most effective and efficient device for delivering social welfare services, what would be the basis of moral objection to their participation in the social market? The relative efficiency and effectiveness of nonprofit- and profit-making-agencies is an issue that moves the debate to grounds of empirical research.

The argument that social welfare programs are better operated by nonprofit agencies than by profit-making enterprises stands on thin grounds empirically. The grounds are thin not because the argument is flimsy but rather because of the immense difficulties of empirical validation. How do we measure the effectiveness of a marital counseling program? By the number of amicable divorces that result, mirthless marriages that are encouraged to persevere, or some more ethereal outcomes such as "greater understanding" (which may lead to more or less happiness) between spouses? Are Planned Parenthood programs to be evaluated according to the number of clients electing to have a specified number of children at certain intervals or to remain childless, to have abortions or to keep their children, or is it simply the provision of information, to whatever end, that defines effectiveness? Are high-quality nursing homes to be measured by attentiveness of the staff, gracious ambience, or the nitty gritty of how many times a week the sheets are changed? Social welfare programs often serve objectives that are impalpable and multiple. The objectives are no less important for these qualities but they frequently defy precise measurement. Many social welfare programs have been studied but relatively few unambiguous measures of effectiveness have been produced.

Negative cases of service outcomes, it seems, are often easier to define and measure than positive results. In this regard the literature is replete with documentation of the failures and abuses of specific agencies. The analysis of proprietary agencies by Rubenstein, Mundy, and Rubenstein, for instance, provides a number of negative examples of practice in profit-making settings as testimony to the inadequacies of these agencies compared to public and nonprofit agencies. The authors do not exaggerate the facts; they are, however, a bit selective in their elaboration. Thus, citing Kenneth Wooden's grim exposé of children's institutions, they note: "One of the more complex and inhumane results of the unconscionable relationship between profit-making in human services and regulation can be seen in the interstate commerce of children. Kenneth Wooden has documented the searing facts of child abuse in Texas proprietary institutions that receive children by the thousands from Illinois, Louisiana, and New Jersey."[20] They neglect to add that Wooden also criticized many public agencies across the country and private nonprofit agencies such as Brother Lester Roloff's infamous Rebekeh Home for girls; even Father Flanagan's Boys Town does not emerge unscathed![21] For those who disapprove of proprietary agency involvement in social welfare it is no doubt tempting to claim that in tallying cases of failure and abuse the weight of evidence provides strong condemnation of profit-making agencies. If only it were so easy. Unfortunately a hard look will uncover sufficient case examples of defects in both profit-making and nonprofit social service agencies to prove conclusively only that shortcomings in dealing with complex and difficult problems of social welfare are widespread.

The relative effectiveness of profit-making and nonprofit social welfare agencies is best judged not by gathering ad hoc examples but by head-on comparative analysis of the performance of similar functions. This is a formidable task. Although many opportunities exist to compare profit-making and nonprofit agencies delivering meals, homemaker, transportation, counseling, day care, and other services, few serious studies have been undertaken on this matter. To glimpse the knottiness of evidence and proof in this realm, one need only review Titmuss's comparative analysis of profit and voluntary nonprofit blood bank systems along with Sapolsky and Finkelstein's critique of this study. Titmuss offers evidence to support the superiority of the voluntary nonprofit system on both ethical and nonethical criteria. The nonethical criteria include efficiency, as measured in less shortage and waste, and quality, as reflected in lower incidence of hepatitis infection transmitted through blood transfusions in the voluntary system.[22] Sapolsky and Finkelstein bring data to bear that seriously challenge the presumed benefits of the nonprofit system. For example, they introduce research findings that show race and ethnicity correlated with the risk of hepatitis infection—northern Europeans having the lowest risk followed by southern Europeans, blacks, and Orientals. Underscoring the significance of racial and ethnic factors, they point to the low transfusion hepatitis rate in Sweden, which pays its donors, compared with the high rate in Japan, which initiated a voluntary system in the late 1960s. In light of these data they conclude that while the voluntary system in Great Britain indeed has a much lower rate of transfusion hepatitis than the profit-oriented system in the United States, those differences may be explained as much by the racial and ethnic stock of the donors as by the paid or voluntary character of their donation.[23]

In regard to the ethical criteria that Titmuss associates with the voluntary nonprofit blood bank system, such as the positive impact on expressions of altruism and the heightened sense of community, the survey data drawn upon to support these conclusions are rather tenuous. (Of the two main questions on altruism reported from Titmuss's survey, the first multiple choice question with no "selfish" or nonvoluntary categories is a bit one-sided, and the second open-ended question appears to suffer from contamination of the first.)[24] These data lend faint support to social work scholars who contend, for example, that Titmuss "demonstrated convincingly that commercialization of blood and donor relationships represses the expression of altruism and erodes the sense of community;"[25] or that "Titmuss has shown that altruism may assure a higher quality product than do market incentives."[26] More to the point, interpretations concerning the extent to which broad sentiments such as altruism and sense of community are influenced by voluntary or commercial blood banks rather than, say, religion, history, culture, and, not least, homogeneity of population, are at best highly speculative exercises, even when conducted with the intellectual prowess and élan that Titmuss brought to this study. Finally, while the gift of blood has a dramatic quality, a gesture more indicative of altruism and social responsibility would oblige one to give something that as Reisman observes, "does not renew itself quite so quickly."[27]

These criticisms notwithstanding, Titmuss's study represents one of the most ambitious and trenchant efforts to assess empirically the relative merits of voluntary and proprietary social welfare arrangements. The indeterminate findings in this significant, though delimited, area of blood transfusion services suggest some of the limits of evaluative research and raise a larger epistemological issue: Given the multiple and often vague character of social welfare goals and the limits of research methods, can enough firm evidence be gathered over an ample range of services to answer with confidence the general question of how well social welfare objectives are served by agencies under profit versus nonprofit auspices? It is an interesting issue, at the moment unresolved.

In the absence of solid empirical evidence on the relative effectiveness of nonprofit versus profit-oriented social welfare agencies, the debate retreats to the high ground of more speculative theoretical considerations. Here the case is made that nonprofit organizations are potentially better suited as service providers, in the sense of being more responsive to the social welfare needs of the community, than profit-oriented organizations on account of several distinguishing features.

In the first place, the structure of governance in nonprofit organizations traditionally involves boards of directors and advisory groups composed of people expected to promote the social welfare interests of the community. To be sure, these board members are often drawn from professional circles and the elite; they are selected in part because their status and influence may enhance fund-raising efforts and provide other organizational benefits; and their definitions of the commonweal do not always coincide with those held by social welfare clients and people from other segments of the community. Still, the central point remains that in setting organizational policy, the governing structure of nonprofit organizations mediates between the public interests of the community being served and the private ends of the organization's members.

Over the past fifteen years a significant increase in client-group-member participation on governing boards of public and private nonprofit social welfare agencies has reinforced the mission and capacity of these bodies to represent the varied interests of the community. This marked change in board composition was perhaps the most important legacy of the citizen participation movements of the 1960s.[28] One might almost say that those movements fashioned a new norm which mandates client-group representation on social welfare agency boards. This development has strengthened agency accountability to both the community at large and the agency's clients within the community.

In contrast to nonprofit organizations, the directorship of profit-making agencies is concerned with protecting the financial interests of the ownership group to which they usually belong. This is as it should be. Investors, staff, and the general public expect the governing bodies of profit-making agencies to act in their self-interest. This is not to say that these bodies are oblivious to community welfare or devoid of public spirit. At the bottom line, however, abstract considerations of these sorts rarely take precedence over the hard and clear requirements of profit-and-loss statements.

Traditionally, profit-making organizations have been held accountable to the consumer public, not through their governing boards but directly over the counter, so to speak. A consumer can go elsewhere if the product or service does not meet the need. This direct link between market transactions and accountability is severed by public purchase-of-service agreements that are used to finance the delivery of social services. With this type of third-party payment the entire transaction is perceived by neither the consumer, who does not pay for the service, nor the purchaser, who does not receive the service. Under these arrangements the service provider is more accountable to the public body purchasing services than to the consumer. As previously noted, however, this indirect line of accountability often travels through two or three layers of government; the information costs are quite high; and the degree of accountability thus achieved is often limited.

In addition to the higher degrees of public accountability vested in the governing boards of public and private nonprofit agencies, the corporate charter of private nonprofit organizations promises that they will be less likely to exploit vulnerable circumstances than profit-making organizations. Nonprofit organizations, despite their label, are not barred from earning a surplus which would normally be considered "profit" in proprietary organizations. Indeed, many nonprofit agencies show a surplus after paying all the annual costs of operation. However, the corporate charter of nonprofit organizations prohibits the distribution of any net earnings among the organization's members; these profits can be used legally only to finance further production of the organization's established services.[29] This constraint against the distribution of profits affords an extra degree of consumer protection in four vulnerable circumstances that often characterize the delivery of social welfare services: These circumstances are: (a) where there is a separation between consumer and purchaser of services as in the third-party payments noted above; (b) where the complexity and nonstandardized character of services, such as marital counseling, child care, and rehabilitation of the physically disabled, make it difficult for consumers to compare and judge their quality and value; (c) where consumer choice is limited because the service involves the exercise of coercive power, as in protective services for children and compulsory admission to a psychiatric hospital; and (d) where alternative services to choose among are simply not available, as in many rural areas in which Hobson's choice is the only one open to consumers. By undermining the conventional discipline of the economic market imposed through competition and consumer choice, these circumstances invite profiteering. In nonprofit agencies the temptation for such abuse is curbed by the legal prohibition against distribution of profits.

Finally a salient distinction between proprietary and nonprofit organizations lies in the motives and ideological disposition characteristic of these enterprises. There is a charitable ethos associated with public and private nonprofit social welfare agencies that stands in contrast to the capitalist spirit of profit-making organizations. "Caveat emptor" may be an appropriate principle to guide business transactions in the market economy. In the field of social welfare, however, where the consumer rarely purchases the service and is often in a vulnerable life situation, the responsibility for regulating the quality of service remains largely in the hands of the providers. It is here that the charitable ethos of nonprofit agencies is likely to exercise a positive influence on the quality of response to social welfare needs. This is neither to say that nonprofit organizations are morally superior nor to imply that the capitalist spirit masks a faintly restrained cupidity, as its detractors are prone to claim. On the contrary, as Max Weber observed, unlimited greed for gain is an impulse quite apart from, even somewhat counter to, the rational and systematic attitude that marks the spirit of capitalism.[30] Still, it is often argued that, even in moderation, the acquisitive drive of profit-oriented agencies unchecked by consumer regulation inherent in market transactions does not offer the best guarantee for meeting social welfare needs. Such a view, for example, prompted the New York City Board of Hospitals to pass regulations governing the minimum floor space per bed, which applied only to proprietary hospitals. When challenged in court, the city argued that it was reasonable to distinguish between profit- and nonprofit-making enterprises "on the grounds that where the profit motive is involved there is a need for regulation to insure that the desire to increase income and cut expenses does not result in dangerous overcrowding and understaffing." While the courts upheld this regulation, one judge's dissenting comments offer the incisive suggestion that in questions of financial motive one might want to consider not only a hospital's profitmaking status, but also the pecuniary interests of its doctors and the animating motives of its trustees.[31]

To some extent the theoretical argument discussed above presents an exaggerated view of the differences between profit- and nonprofit-oriented organizations.[32] Heightened public accountability, the nature of third-party purchasing arrangements, constraints on the distribution of profits, and the charitable ethos apparently grant the clear advantage to nonprofit social welfare providers. If the case seems clear, however, it is only because it is incomplete. A few words are in order to balance the assessment of profit-making versus nonprofit enterprises by examining the opaque realities of this case.

Anyone who has worked in both settings knows that nonprofit agencies are as deeply concerned as profit-oriented ones about maintaining a secure financial position, projecting a positive public image, and other common elements of organizational survival and enhancement, the charitable ethos notwithstanding. Nonprofit board members may represent a broad spectrum of communal interests, but they are not above letting matters of self-interest sometimes intrude on their interpretation of the commonweal.

As for fiscal protection, the prohibition on distribution of profits is a statutory constraint that may be enforced by state attorney generals as well as the Internal Revenue Service. In practice, however, efforts at enforcement are minimal.[33] It is often charged that nonprofit agencies consume through excessive salaries and fringe benefits the surplus financial resources that would become dividends in fiscally more stringent profit-oriented agencies. Allegations of such abuses can be found in many service areas including nursing homes, schools for the handicapped, workshops for the blind, and juvenile institutions.[34]

Even if the nonprofit organization's statutory constraint on distribution of surplus income were policed more vigorously, this is not the only procedure to limit the taking of profits. Alternative devices serving the same function may be adopted for use with profit-making organizations. One such common device is the cost-plus contract, under which purchase-of-service agreements with the government pay private agencies for all the costs of delivering a service plus a specified percentage of profit. Agencies that receive third-party purchase-of-service contracts are relieved from the necessity of competing for consumer fees at the point of service delivery. But purchase-of-service arrangements need not be totally deprived of the benefits of competition among service providers. Some of the discipline imposed by competition may be recouped for both profit and nonprofit agencies under competitive bidding schemes through which contracts can be awarded in the first place, if enough service providers are available to make the bidding a viable contest.[35] Thus, in dealing with both nonprofit and profit-oriented organizations it is theoretically possible to introduce competition and to exercise protective measures against profiteering.

Ethical constraints imposed by the charitable ethos of nonprofit social welfare organizations do not operate with equal force across the range of service providers. Hansmann suggests that these constraints may be stronger in older, and therefore more tradition-bound, sectors than in those that have developed more recently, such as the nursing home industry, which has experienced immense growth over the past few decades. He also observes that ethical constraints may operate more effectively in large organizations than in small ones, since there are more people around to scrutinize the activities.[36] No doubt, nonprofit agencies affiliated with ethnic and religious groups are more likely to sustain the charitable ethos than nonprofit subsidiaries of profit-oriented organizations, which are sometimes created to facilitate entry into social welfare markets limited to nonprofit organizations.

In sum, variations among nonprofit agencies are large, and in dealing with profit- and nonprofit-oriented agencies there is considerable overlap on many dimensions of organizational life.[37] If the theoretical distinctions were drawn more sharply than reality allows, it is only to emphasize the manner in which the essential character of the social market of the welfare state is shaped by norms of public accountability and the charitable ethos. In contrast, regulation through consumer choice and the profit motive are prominent features of transactions in the market economy.

THE ESSENTIAL ISSUE

In weighing the benefits of profit-making versus nonprofit organizations as social service providers, there is probably a range of services in which the relative advantages of either form are marginal. Beyond those cases, in some services the profit form may be superior and in other cases nonprofit agencies may hold the advantage. The essential issue is not to determine the universally superior form of organization, but to understand the particular conditions under which either profit- or nonprofit-oriented agencies may be the most suitable provider of social services.

An examination of the theoretical debate suggests three practical conditions that bear on the choice between profit-making and nonprofit providers for a given service. The first condition is the nature of the service, whether it involves a standardized or custom-tailored product and procedure. It is easier to predict and measure the costs of standardized services, such as public health vaccinations, as well as to monitor their delivery. While amenable to the economic planning skills and business initiative of profit-making organizations, the uniform quality of standardized services also affords the purchaser a favorable chance to evaluate what they are paying for and to control against potential abuses.

The second condition is the average client's degree of competence. Many social services deal with children, the mentally retarded, and confused and emotionally upset people. These client groups are highly vulnerable to exploitation. To the extent that public account-ability and the charitable ethos influence the behavior of nonprofit organizations more than that of profit-making organizations, the nonprofit form is preferable for delivering services to these client groups.

The third condition is whether the service is invested with coer-cive powers. More important than the limits imposed on consumer choice, services that involve the exercise of coercive power pose a significant threat to personal liberty. Where the client's freedom of movement is concerned, the service provider's degree of public accountability is of foremost importance. There is too much at stake here to rely upon the tentative public accountability of profit-making organizations. Even outside the profit-making sector, more imme-diate and direct accountability and, hence, better protection against the misuse of coercive powers are accessible under the auspices of public than private nonprofit service providers.

In general, these three conditions favor public and private non-profit agencies as more fitting providers than profit-making agencies for many types of social services. Yet, there are clearly a variety of services for which this general proposition does not hold. For exam-ple, meals-on-wheels programs, transportation services for the han-dicapped and elderly, telephone reassurance services, and, to a lesser extent, homemaker services which can be divided into standard tasks, satisfy all three conditions in a way that might support the activities of profit-making providers as well as those of nonprofit persuasion.

In recent years the influx of profit-oriented agencies into the wel-fare state has been both rapid and indiscriminate. Yet, there has been relatively little political controversy concerning either specific ques-tions about the types of social welfare services they may be best suited to perform or the general issues of congruity between profit-making activity and social welfare functions. While there are few definitive answers to these questions, their underlying concerns surely merit more vigorous inquiry than has been their due. To understand why concerns of these sorts have been muted, we need only recognize how comfortably profit-oriented agencies fit into the broader frame-work of welfare capitalism that is unfolding in the 1980s—a frame-work resting on the cornerstones of entrepreneuralism, efficiency, and choice.

NOTES

1. Stuart D. Brandes, *American Welfare Capitalism: 1880-1940* (Chicago: University of Chicago Press, 1976), p. 147.

2. Ibid.

3. Richard Crossman, ed., *New Fabian Essays* (London: Turnstile Press, 1952).

4. Robert Pinker, *The Idea of Welfare* (London: Heinemann, 1979), p. 22.

5. T. H. Marshall, "Value Problems of Welfare Capitalism," *Journal of Social Policy*, 1 (1972), 15-32.

6. We might note that recent changes in the British welfare state appear headed to the general direction of those in the United States, though not along the same paths. See, for example, Alan Walker, "A Right Turn for the British Welfare State?" *Social Policy*, 11 (Mar./Apr. 1980), 47-51.

7. Alexis de Tocqueville, *Democracy in America* (New York: Washington Square Press ed., 1964), pp. 181-85.

8. Alex M. Skolnik and Sophie R. Dales, "Social Welfare Expenditures, 1950-1975," *Social Security Bulletin*, 39 (Jan. 1976), 3-20.

9. Neil Gilbert, "The Transformation of Social Services," *Social Service Review* 51 (Dec. 1977), 632-34.

10. Alvin Chenkin, "Government Support to Jewish Sponsored Agencies in Six Major Fields of Service, 1962-73," background paper prepared for the Sidney Hollander Colloquium, Apr. 24 and 25, 1976 (mimeographed).

11. Booze, Allen and Hamilton, *Purchase of Social Service—Study of the Experience of Three States in Purchase of Service by Contract Under the Provisions of the 1967 Amendments to the Social Security Act*, report submitted to the Social and Rehabilitation Service, Jan. 29, 1971, distributed by National Technical Information Service, U.S. Department of Commerce, pp. 40-42.

12. Lester Salamon and Alan Abramson, *The Federal Budget and the Nonprofit Sector* (Washington, D.C.: Urban Institute Press, 1982), p. 44.

13. Ralph Kramer, "Public Fiscal Policy and Voluntary Agencies in Welfare States," *Social Service Review*, 53 (Mar. 1979), 1-14; Felice Perlmutter, "The Effects of Public Funds on Voluntary Sectarian Services," *Journal of Jewish Communal Services*, 45 (Summer 1969) 312-21; Camille Lambert, Jr., and Leah Lambert, "Impact of Poverty Funds on Voluntary Agencies," *Social Work*, 15 (Apr. 1970), 53-61.

14. Subcommittee on Long-Term Care of the Senate Special Committee on Aging, *Nursing Home Care in the United States: Failure in Public Policy, Introductory Report* (Washington, D.C.: U.S. Government Printing Office [GPO], 1974), pp. 20-25.

15. For example, see Joseph Telyveld, "Drive-in Day Care," *New York Times Magazine* (Jan. 5, 1977), p. 110.

16. Pacific Consultants, "Title XX Purchase of Service: A Description of States Service Delivery and Management Practices," Report to the Administration for Public Services, 1978.

17. This point is suggested by Bill Utting, "Purchase of Personal Social Services by Government Agencies in the USA," report to the German Marshall Fund (Dec. 1980).

18. Mary A. Mendelsohn, *Tender Loving Greed* (New York: Knopf, 1974).

19. Henry B. Hansmann, "The Role of Nonprofit Enterprise," *Yale Law Journal*, 89 (Apr. 1980), 880-81.

20. Dan Rubenstein, Richard E. Mundy, and Mary Louise Rubenstein, "Proprietary Social Services," in *The Social Welfare Forum, 1978* (New York: Columbia University Press, 1979), p. 134.

21. Kenneth Wooden, *Weeping in the Playtime of Others* (New York: McGraw-Hill, 1976).

22. Richard Titmuss, *The Gift Relationship* (New York: Pantheon, 1971).

23. Harvey M. Sapolsky and Stan Finkelstein, "Blood Policy Revisited—A New Look at 'The Gift Relationship,'" *Public Interest*, 46 (Winter 1977), 15–27.

24. Titmuss, *Gift Relationship*, pp. 306–15.

25. Kurt Reichert, "The Drift Toward Entrepreneurialism in Health and Social Welfare: Implications for Social Work Education," *Administration in Social Work*, 1 (Summer 1977), 129.

26. Alfred J. Kahn, *Social Policy and Social Services* (New York: Random House, 1973), pp. 148–49.

27. D. A. Reisman, *Richard Titmuss: Welfare and Society* (London: Heinemann, 1977), p. 109.

28. Harry Specht, "The Grass Roots and Government in Social Planning and Community Organization," *Administration in Social Work*, 2 (Fall 1978), 319–34.

29. For a detailed analysis of the "nondistribution constraint" see Hansmann, "Role of Nonprofit Enterprise."

30. Max Weber, *The Protestant Ethic and the Spirit of Capitalism*, trans. Talcott Parsons (New York: Scribner, 1958), p. 1.

31. Engelsher v. Jacobs, 184 New York Supplemental, 2d 640 (1959).

32. For an analysis of this question from an administrative perspective, see James D. Thompson, "Pittsburgh Committee Report on Common and Uncommon Elements in Administration," in *Social Work Administration*, ed. Harry Schatz (New York: Council on Social Work Education, 1970), pp. 30–41.

33. Kenneth Karst, "The Efficiency of the Charitable Dollar: An Unfulfilled State Responsibility," 73, *Harvard Law Review* (1960), 433–83.

34. See, for example, "Levitt Audit Finds Overpayments to Private Schools for the Handicapped," *New York Times*, Dec. 18, 1977, p. 76; Wooden, *Weeping in the Playtime*; Mendelsohn, *Tender Loving Greed*; and *Wall Street Journal*, Jan. 24, 1979, p.1, col. 1.

35. Competitive bidding for social service contracts is rare. For an example of this approach and some lessons that were drawn from the experience in Hennepin County, see Donald Fisk, Herbert Kiesling, and Thomas Muller, *Private Provision of Public Services: An Overview* (Washington, D.C.: Urban Institute Press, 1978), pp. 54–57.

36. Hansmann, "Role of Nonprofit Enterprise," p. 876

37. Some analysts suggest that the profit-versus-nonprofit classification may be less significant than other variables, such as size, goals, and domains, for comprehending organizational behavior. For discussion of this position see Paul J. Gordon, "Managing Diverse Organizational Strategies," Richard M. Cyert, *The Management of Nonprofit Organizations* (Lexington, Mass.: Lexington Books, 1975), pp. 102–05.

TWO

ENTREPRENEURS, EFFICIENCY, AND CHOICE

The penetration of profit-oriented agencies into the welfare state imbues the social market with the spirit of capitalism and inclines the modus operandi of social welfare transactions toward that of the market economy. The appearance of profit-making agencies in the welfare state is not the only indication of this trend. Movement toward commercialization of the social market is evident in a variety of activities throughout the welfare state, ranging from the behavior of front line professionals responsible for service delivery to the plans and actions of public funding sources.

WELFARE PROFESSIONALS AND THE ENTREPRENEURIAL INSTINCT

Although the welfare state includes programs run by people from many related professions, social work is clearly the major source of trained personnel in this area and is involved with the broadest range of social welfare programs. Since the early 1960s entrepreneurial ambitions have been spreading among welfare professionals, particularly the membership of the National Association of Social Workers (NASW), which represents the main body of professional social work. While social work practice traditionally has been agency based, between 1967 and 1975 the number of NASW members engaged in private practice more than doubled from approximately 3,500 to 8,500.[1]

Social work's professional origins go back to the friendly visiting activities sponsored by Charity Organization Societies in the late nineteenth century. As they were formalized, these activities came to be called the practice of "applied philanthropy." The New York School of Applied Philanthropy, established in 1898, was the first school of social work in the United States. The ideological grain of social work's philanthropic heritage runs counter to fee-for-service activities and the profit motive, which characterize private practice in the market economy. Indeed, in the 1920s private practice was discouraged under the policies of the American Association of Social Workers, which later merged with other social work organizations to form the NASW.[2]

Despite ideological reservations, private practice holds considerable appeal for many social workers. It is seen as a way to free professional practice from the bureaucratic constraints of agency settings. Cast in opposition to bureaucratic obstructions to service delivery rather than in pursuit of profit-oriented activity, attractions to private practice assume the moral legitimacy of being in the client's best interest. One argument, drawing upon the market economy doctrine, asserts that clients would additionally benefit from heightened competition among independent service providers, as social work practice shifted from bureaucratic to entrepreneurial enterprises.[3] In the bargain there are, of course, increased professional recognition and financial rewards as an extra fillip to private practice. In regard to financial rewards, over the last two decades the growing prospects for reimbursement of social work services through third-party vendor payments provided by public and private health insurance schemes have intensified the lure of private practice.

The legitimacy of private social work practice was formally acknowledged in 1962, when the NASW Delegate Assembly adopted an interim set of minimum standards that applied to private practice. In 1964 a position statement was issued bestowing NASW's official stamp of approval as follows: "The National Association of Social Workers recognizes private practice as a legitimate area of social work, but it affirms that practice in socially sponsored organizational structures must remain the primary avenue for the implementation of the goals of the profession."[4] This position statement reflects social work's effort to reconcile its historical commitment to serving the disadvantaged through agencies in the social market with a recently increasing entrepreneurial orientation among its membership; the result is a transparent compromise in which NASW endorses private practice while urging its containment. Despite the equivocation of this endorsement, NASW's position lends impetus to the new direction toward which welfare capitalism has been evolving over the last decade.

More recently, the entrepreneurial attraction to private practice has been joined by an increasing interest in another aspect of the market economy—the provision of social services in the work place. In 1976 the National Association of Social Workers in cooperation with the Council on Social Work Education sponsored a three-year nationwide project to study and develop materials on industrial social work. Toward the mid-1970s industrial social work had become a rapidly growing field of practice. Between 1972 and 1978 approximately 2,000 employee assistance programs were established under the auspices of private enterprise.[5] By 1980 more than 5,000 of these programs were operating nationwide, offering employees a range of social services to help them deal with marital, alcohol, drug, emotional, family, legal, financial, and job-related problems.[6]

As proprietary agencies have discovered a potential market for expansion in the welfare state, so too welfare professionals have lit upon a market for their services in private industry. And just as there are certain strains (discussed in chap. 1) between the way proprietary agencies function and the mechanics of the social market, so too the values and objectives of social work professionals are not in complete harmony with those of private industry.[7] The dissonance in this field of practice echoes back to earlier experiences.

Despite the contemporary surge of interest, industrial social work is not a new calling. It flourished briefly under the initial phase of welfare capitalism sponsored by American business at the turn of the twentieth century.[8] In 1919 a Bureau of Labor Statistics survey revealed that social or welfare secretaries (as the first industrial social workers were called) were employed by almost three-quarters of 431 of the largest companies in the United States. Industry attracted more graduates of the New York School of Social Work class of 1920 than any other setting.[9] By the 1930s, however, welfare secretaries had virtually disappeared from the industrial scene, many functions of their work having been incorporated into the emerging profession of personnel management.[10]

Industrial social workers of the 1920s were agents of management. They provided employees various types of social assistance and in the process exercised a highly paternalistic form of social control. Their objectives were to enhance employee well-being while improving the stability and productivity of the work force. When social work's humanistic concern for employee well-being came into conflict with industry's desire for increased productivity, the latter ultimately determined the outcome. Thus, in one sense the evolution of welfare secretaries away from social work and toward personnel management can be seen as a resolution of the inherent strain between social work's humanistic commitments and the economic values of industry. With the recent revival of industrial social work that strain is bound to reappear, creating further pressure for welfare professionals to adopt the doctrine of the market economy.

The advent of government-financed purchase of service and third-party vendor payments and the growing number of employee assistance programs in private industry have no doubt stimulated entrepreneurial ambitions among welfare professionals traditionally employed by public and private nonprofit agencies. However, the movement toward the fee-for-service model of private practice and industrial social work is a response to many factors beyond the increasing opportunities opened by government and industrial financing. The enhanced professional status associated with private practice and the battering that "good works" under philanthropic auspices suffered during the social upheavals of the late 1960s also influenced this development.

While gaining popularity in the United States, private practice is not the only avenue for expression of the entrepreneurial spirit among welfare professionals. Within the bureaucratic context of agency-based practice British social welfare planners have devised an interesting scheme to tap the energies and resourcefulness associated with entrepreneurial activity. The prototype for this scheme is the Kent Community Care Project. Addressing the problems of long-term care, the Kent project was designed to provide a network of support services that would delay or avoid institutionalization of the frail elderly. Three propositions guided the design of this project: (1) Often the frail elderly are institutionalized not because such placement is the most socially and cost-effective solution to their problems but because of the rigidity of social service provider roles and conventional procedures that inhibit the provision of a suitable mix of supports necessary for the elderly to remain in the community; (2) with some imagination and the flexible deployment of resources social workers could weave tailor-made networks of service to support many frail elderly in the community at a higher level of personal well-being and a lower cost to the public than would result from placement in an institution; (3) to achieve flexibility, resourceful-ness, and cost-effective outcomes social workers should be given discretion over allocation of a budget for each client, the size of which is not expected to exceed two-thirds the cost of institutional place-ment, along with detailed information on the unit costs of alternative service arrangements.[11]

In exercising control over client budget allocations, social workers can purchase all sorts of supports to interweave with existing statutory services and informal care provided by family members. For example, they may have a telephone installed in the client's home, buy the client a number of meals weekly at a local restaurant, and pay neigh-bors to assist the client during those times such as evenings, week-ends, and holidays, when conventional home help services are nor-mally unavailable. By providing information on the unit costs of alternative resources and limiting expenditures on each client to two-thirds the rate for institutional placement, the Kent project en-courages social workers to make the "best deal" in purchasing and otherwise mobilizing services to fit the client's special needs and circumstances. These features of the scheme allow some latitude for entrepreneurial initiative to flourish within an agency-based setting.

THE DRIVE FOR EFFICIENCY

At the same time that welfare professionals are cultivating their entre-preneurial instincts, public funding agencies have put increasing pressure on service providers to improve the efficiency of social welfare programs. This development was set in motion during the Nixon administration, when old-line professional social welfare leaders in the Department of Health, Education and Welfare (HEW) were replaced by management-oriented officials, whose first act was a strenuous campaign to reduce error rates in public assistance. The emphasis on efficiency has continued as reflected in the Office of Human Development Services 1980 research priorities, which in-cludes the question: How can business skills be applied within public organizations to increase the efficiency and effectiveness of public services?[12]

Without the discipline that competition imparts, the welfare state has long been exposed to public suspicion of inefficiency. The benevolent ethos of welfare agencies may further contribute to this impression, since the idea of "efficient benevolence" sounds faintly contradictory. As the market economy doctrine gains adherents in the welfare state, social service agencies are being asked to behave in a more "businesslike" manner, which Peter Drucker observes, usually translates "to little more than control of costs."[13] Given the difficulty of evaluating exactly what many social welfare programs achieve, funding sources naturally turn to comparisons of how much it costs to run a program and support the most efficient operations. It is, of course, quite reasonable to require agencies in the social market to operate as efficiently as possible. Indeed, efficient administration of relief was a prominent mission of the Charity Organization Societies, precursors of the voluntary sector in the modern welfare state. In stressing the "scientific" approach to charity, these early welfare agencies sought to reduce the inefficient allocation of community resources that resulted from indiscriminate giving.

Yet efficiency can be a deceptive criterion for comparing programs in the social market, where consumer choice is limited and measures of effectiveness are complex and difficult to obtain. Here surrogate outcomes, such as number of clients served, often displace assessments of substantive benefits, creating an arbitrary base against which to measure efficiency.[14] In almost any social welfare program there is a significant range between minimal and optimal provisions. For example, nutrition projects for the elderly serve an average of 450,000 meals daily, most of them in congregate dining facilities provided by senior centers throughout the country[15]; on a culinary scale of taste and presentation these meals probably rate as more appealing than army rations and less splendid than haute cuisine. If the efficiency of these programs were judged on the easily measured criteria of nutrition and numbers served, the tendency toward menus on the lower end of the culinary scale would eventually prevail. Moreover, other benefits of the programs, particularly "soft" ones such as the opportunity for social contact, would be overlooked if not diminished. The amenities of a cozy sociable atmosphere are costlier to keep up than the bleak dining hall environment of a Bowery mission.

Nutrition projects for the elderly are not a special case. Wherever there is some slack in the definition of social welfare program objectives and uncertainty around performance measures, the standard of efficiency perforce pushes in the direction of minimal provisions: child development programs slide toward routine baby-sitting operations, planned parenthood toward pill dispensing, nursing homes toward human warehousing, and so forth.[16] Ronald Randall cites the extreme case of an official reporting on one state's successful efforts to reduce error rates on diabetic diet allowances: "They no longer allow special diabetic diet allowances."[17]

Eliminating program benefits to reduce error rates is a grotesque strategy. On more typical grounds, however, the drive for efficiency has led beyond minimal provisions to proposals for what are stintingly labeled "nonservice approaches" to social welfare.[18] The essential characteristic of various nonservice approaches is that they seek to augment and extend social welfare arrangements without direct government spending. They are mirrored in recommendations that the Reagan administration follow the "least cost" path in managing the Office of Human Development Services. This path "should consist of approaches outside the traditional 'social work' framework," such as employing tax reforms instead of developing new social services to address social welfare problems.[19] In general, nonservice approaches depend upon the government's ability to tax, regulate, and collaborate with private enterprise, induce administrative reforms, and encourage self-help.

Proponents of nonservice approaches suggest the following examples of how they may work:[20]

1. Deregulation of zoning and building code requirements affecting day-care centers can be used to stimulate the supply of family providers who care for a number of children in their own home, usually at a lower cost than in larger institutions. Similarly, by waiving codes governing single-family zones, "granny flats" built out of prefabricated modules designed for easy attachment to existing structures can be erected as a convenient method for housing elderly parents.

2. Policies regarding property taxes can be fashioned to protect low-income homeowners by introducing a "circuit breaker" which automatically shuts off taxes when they reach a designated

percentage of the homeowners' income. Nearly three-fourths of the states have circuit breaker tax policies for elderly home-owners.

3. Administrative procedures may be changed to allow for alternative utilization of public facilities, particularly school buildings that often stand empty in afternoons and the summer months.

4. Government can urge private sector enterprises to contribute goods, services, facilities, and financial assistance to social ser-vices in their communities. This kind of private sector involvement may include donating unsalable surplus food to community food banks; lending vans used by private firms for morning and evening commuters as backup vehicles during the day for Dial-a-Ride services to the elderly; and allowing private cafeteria facilities to be used between working hours to prepare food for meals-on-wheels programs.

5. Public social service programs can stimulate local self-help efforts through the recruitment and training of volunteers. Numerous voluntary activities, such as visits to the elderly and cooperative child-care arrangements, currently supplement and enrich exist-ing service networks.

6. Private lending institutions can design and finance reverse annuity mortgages that allow elderly homeowners to convert the equity in their homes into disposable income. It is estimated that in 1980, elderly homeowners had about $500 billion of untapped equity locked up in their homes.[21] Home equity conversion plans allow the low-income elderly to "unlock" this equity and to supplement their income without having to sell their homes. A variety of these plans are being tested across the country.[22]

Despite the implicit promise of cutting new paths, most of the proposals for nonservice approaches travel along fairly conventional routes. In the main they aim at creating highly efficient social welfare delivery systems by stretching available resources and supplement-ing services with low-cost alternatives. In practice these strategies bear careful scrutiny. If resources are stretched too thin, hidden costs may erupt. Deregulation of zoning and building codes, for example, may stimulate the production of low-cost day-care services by family providers in private homes at the same time that they increase uncertainty and, perhaps, even an element of risk concerning the health, safety, and quality of these arrangements. That is, of course, assuming that building code regulations bear some relationship to promoting the health and safety of occupants. Moreover, one reason private homes are less expensive than large institutional day-care programs is that they usually are not equipped to offer more than limited forms of baby-sitting service while institutional programs often engage in broad child development activities, which brings us back to the problem of grasping for easily measured standards of efficiency in the absence of subtler and more complex measures of program effectiveness—a situation in which decisionmakers learn the price of everything and the value of nothing.

Without clearly defined measures of program performance there is no firm base upon which to judge standards of efficiency. The cry for better measures of program performance (at least with respect to the "quality" of social welfare programs, if not their ultimate effectiveness) echoed in the halls of HEW throughout the 1970s. And it has been getting louder as professional journals, associations, and consulting firms dedicated to program evaluation have multiplied and added their voices to the call.

Efforts to tap program performance in the welfare state have turned to measures of consumer satisfaction or preference.[23] The assumptions underlying this move are compatible with the current ideological directions of welfare capitalism. In essence the approach is to ask social welfare clients to express their satisfaction with services "as if" they were shopping in the marketplace. With some squinting these measures can be seen as a way to approximate the market criterion of consumer choice in a competitive environment where the "better mouse trap" will prevail over those of lesser quality.

While this method for judging the performance of social welfare programs is attuned to prevailing themes of the new welfare capitalism, there are some discordant questions about its cost and validity that deserve closer examination. On the matter of cost, surveys would have to be taken periodically. A study by the Urban Institute, for example, suggests that citizen surveys be conducted regularly by local governments to assist in judging program performance.[24] There are approximately 60,000 local governments in the United States (excluding school districts), few of which have in-house capacity to conduct social surveys. If acted upon, such a recommendation would clearly be a boon to the evaluative research industry. It is less clear how much knowledge would be gained about program performance or efficiency because the results of surveys on social welfare consumer preferences and satisfactions are exceedingly difficult to interpret. These interpretations are complicated by the fact that a number of studies have found little relationship between professional assessments of the slender objective indicators of service quality that are available and ratings of consumer satisfaction.[25] When surveyed, consumers generally respond with favorable assessments of staff and services.[26] This tendency to express satisfaction with social welfare services has been variously attributed to client gratitude and politeness, a natural inclination to rationalize one's involvement in a program as a worthwhile activity, and the adaptation of client expectations to the existing level of services.[27] Whatever the reason, there is much evidence to suggest that, despite the sophisticated statistical manipulations often accompanying client surveys, the translation of consumer satisfaction ratings into judgments of social welfare program performance is an exercise of dubious validity.

EXPANDING CONSUMER CHOICE

Although consumer preference surveys imply the exercise of choice, it is in a sense the absence of actual choice in the social market that prompts public efforts to evaluate program performance through this method. The alternative is to supplant the public provision of social welfare services by tax credits, vouchers, and cash grants, which would enable consumers to purchase services of their choice on the private market. The 1976 amendments to the Internal Revenue Code, for example, introduced tax credits of up to $800 for child-care expenses incurred by families in which parents are working or in school. Cash provisions allow consumers to register their preferences not on the vague checklists of social surveys but with direct payment for services rendered. Proponents of this approach claim that it stimulates competition and would impose a form of discipline on the welfare state functionally equivalent to that operating in the market economy. Presumably, this discipline would enhance social service efficiency, accountability, and innovation.

Both vouchers and tax credits have a structured exchange value. Tax credits for child care, food stamps, and educational vouchers each can be used to purchase goods or services within a designated sector. They are of little value outside their respective sectors except on the black market, where certain vouchers such as food stamps sometimes are illegally exchanged for cash at a discount rate. Theoretically, vouchers and tax credits function in a similar fashion, preserving ample latitude for consumer choice (within sectors), while allowing public agencies a degree of social control over consumption patterns, which offers ultimate assurance that the benefits will serve their socially defined purposes. The main practical differences between vouchers and tax credits are the methods of distribution and the populations they have an impact upon. Vouchers are certificates of monetary value distributed by social welfare agencies prior to the purchase of designated goods and services. Tax credits are distributed after the purchase through the reduction of income taxes by the Internal Revenue Service. To benefit from tax credits one must have enough money on hand for the initial purchase and be in a high enough income bracket to owe taxes against which the full credit may be charged. Aside from these practical differences there is a larger philosophical question (discussed in chap. 8) about whether fiscal measures such as tax credits should be thought of as equivalent to directly subsidized provisions such as food stamps.

Following the trend toward commercialization of the social market, income and voucher schemes have been widely endorsed as alternatives to government's direct provision of services. Food stamps are a classic example of how vouchers operate to expand consumer choice while channeling social welfare provisions through the market economy. Prior to the 1960s the poor could supplement their diets by participating in the Commodity Distribution Program, through which free food was handed out at various centers in the states. Since the 1960s relief in this area has shifted from offering a small selection of food commodities at a limited number of distribution centers to the provision of food stamps that may be used to purchase almost any edible item at local supermarkets. The Food Stamp Program had its origin in a pilot project established by executive order in 1961. This project, which served fewer than 400,000 persons, was expanded to a program of national scope under the

Food Stamp Act of 1964. Between 1967 and 1978 the average number of monthly participants leaped from approximately 1.5 million to 16 million. While this rapid increase in the size and cost of the program has dampened political support for food stamps (see chap. 4), the basic idea of social provisions through vouchers and cash rather than direct services has continued to gain adherents.

During the 1970s three major social experiments were conducted to test consumer-oriented voucher and cash schemes in the areas of education, housing, and income maintenance. Although the experiments did not yield a conclusive verdict about the efficiency and effectiveness of these initiatives, some of the results are thought provoking.

The idea for educational vouchers was introduced by Milton Friedman in 1955.[28] His proposal was simple and direct. Instead of giving money to public schools, government would provide parents with vouchers equal to the average cost of educating their child in the public school system; these vouchers could be used to purchase education at any public or private school of the parent's choice; and parents could add their own funds to the voucher if they wished to send their children to schools that charged more than the average cost of public education. Placing no restrictions on parents or schools, this approach gives free rein to the market mechanisms of consumer choice and competition. A somewhat more restrictive plan for educational vouchers was drawn up by Jencks and his associates in 1970.[29] They also aimed to shake the educational system loose of public bureaucracies but were not as content as Friedman to let the chips fall where they might in the open market. Instead the Jencks plan sought to ensure against racial and economic discrimination through a series of regulations governing admissions policies, fiscal incentives for schools to accept poor students, and the creation of an educational voucher agency to oversee the program and provide parents with information that would enhance the intelligent exercise of choice.

When the Office of Economic Opportunity (OEO) sought to launch an experimental voucher project in 1970, it was Jencks's rather than Friedman's approach they selected to test. In most of the prospective test sites, OEO efforts to promote the voucher project were met with a considerable lack of enthusiasm by both local educators and grass-roots organizations.[30] After several unsuccessful attempts, OEO finally obtained a test site for their voucher demonstration at the Alum Rock Union Elementary School District in San Jose, California. The Alum Rock demonstration ran for five years from 1972 to 1977. In the process of implementation at Alum Rock the voucher concept was drastically modified; choice was limited to 13 of the district's 24 public schools that elected to participate; enrollment ceilings were used to place restriction on demands; instead of going entirely to the school at which a pupil enrolled, almost one-third of the basic voucher was automatically deducted to pay for centralized administrative services; and the cutting edge of competition was sheathed in assurances that no one would lose their teaching job if their program was unsuccessful in attracting consumers.[31]

Despite breaching several principles of the voucher concept, the Alum Rock demonstration did promote a degree of consumer choice and competition beyond that normally operating in the school district. Recognizing that this demonstration did not test a pure voucher scheme, the results are nevertheless suggestive. On the matter of consumer choice, diverse programs were generated by the Alum Rock experiment. While the range of substantive educational alternatives among which parents might select thus increased substantially, in the actual exercise of choice geographical proximity appeared the predominant consideration for most parents. More than 80% chose to send their children to the nearest school. Choices made among different miniprograms within schools tended to favor traditional curricula with high-income families disproportionately represented among the minority selecting nontraditional programs. Finally, in making their choices parents received almost all their information about the school programs directly from the schools.[32]

One of the critical questions about vouchers is whether the quality of education benefits from the competition and choice stimulated by this approach. Weighty issues of this sort are subject to varying interpretations and the Alum Rock experience was no exception. Drawing on findings from Rand's major study of Alum Rock, Milton and Rose Friedman accentuate the positive. They observe that although the demonstration was hardly a proper test of vouchers, at the McCollam School, "giving the parents greater choice had a major effect on the quality of education. In terms of test scores, the McCollam School went from thirteenth to second place among the schools in its district."[33]

Other data from the Rand study suggest that in all the demonstration schools the overall effects were negligible, if not negative. Comparing changes in Metropolitan Achievement Test (MAT) scores for voucher and nonvoucher schools, Barker found no significant difference after the first year.[34] Another Rand investigator examining changes in Cooperative Primary Reading Test (CPRT) scores discovered poorer performance in voucher programs than in nonvoucher programs[35]; these findings were supported and refined in a reanalysis of data on CPRT scores by researchers outside Rand.[36] After three years a second study of student achievement on the MATs again revealed no significant differences between voucher and nonvoucher schools.[37] While these studies are open to criticism on a number of points, the bulk and consistency of evidence raise serious questions about the benefits of diversity and choice under the Alum Rock version of educational vouchers.

In contrast to the voucher form of payment in the Alum Rock demonstration, the Experimental Housing Allowance Program (EHAP) provided benefits through direct cash grants. Launched in 1970, the EHAP was social experimentation on an unprecedented scale; it covered 30,000 households at 12 sites across the country and was executed over an 11-year period at a total cost of about $160 million. One of the central objectives of this experiment was to assess the impact that housing allowances would have upon patterns of housing consumption. Pittsburgh and Phoenix were the sites chosen to explore this issue. At each of these sites 1,800 low-income households were selected to receive housing allowance grants ranging from $38 to $95 per month for three years. Unlike vouchers that are redeemable only in purchasing the types of benefits for which they are intended, the cash grants awarded as housing allowances could be spent on anything. In an effort to channel these cash payments toward housing-related purchases they were obliquely "earmarked" by two kinds of minimum housing consumption requirements. One group of recipients qualified for allowance payments only if their housing met a set of minimum standards, which included the presence of adequate plumbing, heating, and electrical systems, and an occupancy rate of no more than two persons for each bedroom; a second group of recipients was required to maintain specified levels of rental expenditures. The experiment also involved an "unconstrained" group, which received the allowance in the absence of any consumption requirements, and a control group, which was similar in socioeconomic status to the other participants but received no allowance.[38]

What stands out most among the findings of this experiment is the fact that very small amounts of the housing allowances were actually spent on housing. An average of 10% of the payments in Pittsburgh and 25% in Phoenix were used to increase housing consumption.[39] Participants whose dwelling units initially did not meet the program's minimum housing standards showed the largest increase in housing consumption. However, the overall effects of using these housing requirements to earmark cash payments was slight.[40]

For most of the EHAP participants housing allowances became principally an income supplement. The same end could be achieved perhaps more effectively by simply increasing the cash benefits available through existing income maintenance programs such as Aid to Families with Dependent Children (AFDC) and Supplemental Security Income (SSI). This direct cash supplement approach would avoid the extra administrative costs of a special housing allowance program, dodge the confusion of how to treat one program's benefits in determining eligibility for another program, and result in a unified welfare system that is comprehensible to both clients and the public-at-large. Carrying this notion a bit further Milton and Rose Friedman have argued that *all* specific social welfare programs should be replaced by a single comprehensive program of income supplements in cash.[41] They suggest that such a program might take the form of a negative income tax administered by the Internal Revenue Service, which would dispense with much of the current welfare bureaucracy and eliminate the stigma generally associated with public assistance.

A negative income tax program would provide a guaranteed level of financial support for all families. Numerous designs for this type of program have been advanced. These designs vary in two central features: the size of the guaranteed minimum subsidy for families with no income and the negative tax rate that determines the amount by which this basic subsidy decreases as earned income increases.[42]

One of the most perplexing questions about negative income tax proposals is the impact of different negative tax rates on incentives to work. For each dollar of earned income, how would a 50-, 60-, or 70-cent reduction in the basic subsidy affect a worker's motivation to labor for an extra dollar? And how would these effects differ for subsidies offering low, medium, and high levels of support?

These questions, along with others (see chap. 5), were addressed in the Seattle and Denver Income Maintenance Experiments (SIME/DIME), the largest and most carefully controlled income maintenance experiments in history. In brief, this study drew on a sample of 4,706 families, 44 percent of which were assigned to the control group and the remainder divided among 11 experimental groups. Each experimental group received one of three guaranteed levels of support—$3,800, $4,800, and $5,600—and was taxed at varying rates. Four tax rates were used: two involved a constant tax of 50 and 70%, and two involved taxes that started at 70 and 80% and declined as income increased. The Seattle program began in 1970 and Denver in 1971 with participants enrolled for either three or five years.

Findings from SIME/DIME reveal that while changes in work effort varied with the support level and tax rate, in most cases there was a large reduction in the annual hours of work by participating families. An estimate of the nationwide effects of this program indicates that with a guaranteed level of support at 75% of the poverty line and a negative tax rate of 50% the expected reduction in work effort would be about 6% for husbands, 23% for wives, and 7% for female heads of families.[43] There are several reasons to believe that these findings underestimate the reduction in work effort that would actually result if a nationwide guaranteed minimum income program were implemented. The extensive personal attention given to participants made them highly susceptible to an experimental phenomenon known as the Hawthorne effect. This phenomenon suggests that in the process of becoming actively engaged in the experiment the participants would develop a commitment to its success and would behave in ways that would not disappoint the investigators. The limited scale of the experiment could not capture the effects of a nationwide program with millions of participants who might well form an organization to promote negative tax benefits and to encourage others to join their ranks. The relatively brief duration of the experiment no doubt placed a greater restraint on tendencies to reduce work effort significantly and risk losing a job than if the minimum income were permanently guaranteed by the federal government. There is also a likelihood that a guaranteed minimum income would encourage early retirement. Weighting these and other factors, Martin Anderson has developed a series of estimates to correct for biases in the experimental measurement of work reduction. According to his calculations, a guaranteed income would result in a minimum of a 29% reduction in the work effort of low-income workers.[44]

Despite the generally unpersuasive, if not inauspicious, results of the educational voucher, housing, and income maintenance experiments, the movement to expand consumer choice through vouchers, tax credits, and cash grants continues to draw support. In 1979 the Coons and Sugarman proposal for a voucher plan to replace public education in California received a fair amount of public encouragement.[45] Although this proposal failed to qualify for the 1980 California ballot, it remains a politically viable option for the future.[46] Several bills have been put before Congress in the early 1980s for the provision of a tax credit for private education. Tax credits for child-care expenses, as mentioned earlier, were enacted in 1976. In the realm of housing the presidential budget for 1983 proposes to shift assistance for the poor away from provisions in-kind toward a voucher program. These examples reflect the ascending faith in consumer sovereignty as the means and the market economy as the arena for the provision of social welfare in the 1980s. It is a faith that will ultimately serve some people better than others.

When consumer choice in the welfare state is increased, the weight of judgment and responsibility for social welfare is transferred from communal agencies to individual hands. The strength of this approach rests to a large extent on the view of consumer behavior as rational, contemplative, and selective; that is also the weakness in its application to the social market of the welfare state. Consumers of social welfare services traditionally have consisted of the poor, frail aged, handicapped, orphaned, ill educated, mentally disabled, and people otherwise in deep trouble. Lack of knowledge, poor health, and the press of necessity are conditions that impair the competent exercise of consumer choice. In the social market these conditions are often magnified by the difficulty of evaluating complex human services and by the magnitude of the risk attendant upon poor choices. A mistake in selecting, for example, a day-care center, a nursing home, or a mental health agency that provides substandard services has more severe consequences than a bad choice in an average commercial transaction. The major beneficiaries of greater choice would not be the traditional clientele of the welfare state but rather consumers from the middle and working classes, to whom social welfare entitlements have been extended in recent years, a development examined more closely in the next chapter.

THE EMERGING PATTERN

The introduction of profit-oriented units and the growing emphases on efficiency, consumer choice, and entrepreneurial activity are inter-laced threads of thought and action that form the pattern of welfare capitalism emerging in the 1980s. As this pattern unfolds, significant changes are in store for the welfare state, many of which are already in motion. These changes aim for a more coherent, innovative, and accountable system—lean in waste and brisk in the conduct of its affairs—than the current array of well-meaning programs built upon the liberal consensus that influenced public policy from the New Deal to the Great Society. As that consensus crumbled in the 1970s, so has support declined for the social market of the welfare state, with a consequent renewal of faith in principles of the market economy.

To have some reservations about the impetus toward profit, effi-ciency, entrepreneurial activity, and choice in the welfare state and to raise some questions about their presumed benefits is not to dismiss the potential of this movement for positive gains. On the contrary, there is much here that deserves serious consideration. In some areas of social service, such as transportation for the handicapped and residential repair for the elderly, profit-oriented agencies may well be superior to nonprofit agencies. There is probably a range of services for which the profit-versus-nonprofit distinction is inconsequential. The type of entrepreneurial activity practiced by welfare profession-als in the British experiment in community care has attractive features that might easily be incorporated into standard operations of the social market. While the zeal for efficiency may often result in cutting too close to the bone of meaningful social provisions, the welfare state tends to produce a margin of waste that requires frequent trimming somehow. As for consumer choice, it presents opportunities that some social welfare client groups are better able than others to turn to their advantage; there is little reason not to encourage expanding choice for those client groups to whom it is best suited. Separately, in moderate dosage, and with selective application, elements of the capitalist doctrine can no doubt invigorate the welfare state.

Just as the social market can accommodate a measured degree of capitalist doctrine, there is a point beyond which the balance tips against the essential nature of the welfare state. The welfare state of the 1980s is drifting toward this point because in the flurry of expansion between 1960 and 1980 its liberal proponents lost sight of some critical limits. How these limits were overstepped by enlarging the scope and purpose of the social market and the consequences of this development are vividly illustrated in the plight of universal social services.

NOTES

1. Kurt Reichert, "The Drift Toward Entrepreneurialism in Health and Social Welfare: Implications for Social Work Education," *Administration in Social Work*, 2 (Fall 1978), 123–32; Arnold M. Levin, "Private Practice is Alive and Well," *Social Work*, 21 (Sept. 1976), 356–62; Estelle Gabriel, "Private Practice in Social Work," in *Encyclopedia of Social Work* (Washington, D.C.: National Association of Social Workers, 1977), pp. 1054–59.

2. David Hardcastle, "The Profession: Professional Organizations, Licensing, and Private Practice," in *Handbook of the Social Services*, ed. Neil Gilbert and Harry Specht (Englewood Cliffs: Prentice-Hall, 1981), pp. 683–85.

3. Ibid.; for an elaboration of assumptions both in support of and in opposition to private practice see Neil Gilbert, "Assessing Service Delivery Methods: Some Unsettled Questions," *Welfare in Review*, 10 (May/June 1973), 25–33.

4. *Handbook on the Private Practice of Social Work* (Washington, D.C.: National Association of Social Workers, 1974), p. 40.

5. William Sennenstuhl and James E. O'Donnell, "EAPs: The Why's and How's of Planning Them," *Personnel Administrator* (Nov. 1980), pp. 35–38.

6. James T. Wrich, *The Employee Assistance Program* (Center City, Minn.: Hazelden Foundation, 1980). Estimates in 1982 indicate that approximately 8,000 of these programs were in operation throughout the country. See Paul Roman, "Pitfalls of 'Program' Concepts in the Development and Maintenance of Employee Assistance Programs," *Urban and Social Change Review* 16 (Winter 1983), 9.

7. See, for example, Rosalie Bakalinsky, "People vs. Profits: Social Work in Industry," *Social Work*, 25 (Nov. 1980), 471–75.

8. Stuart D. Brandes, *American Welfare Capitalism: 1880–1940* (Chicago: University of Chicago Press, 1976), pp. 111–18.

9. Philip R. Popple, "Social Work Practice in Business and Industry, 1875–1930," *Social Service Review*, 55 (June 1981), 260.

10. Cyril Ling, *The Management of Personnel Relations: History and Origins* (Homewood, Ill.: Richard D. Irwin, 1965).

11. Interim results indicate that compared to a control group the well-being of clients served by the Kent project improved, while project costs were similar, if not lower, than those of conventional provisions received by the control group. See Bleddyn Davies and David Challis, "Experimenting with New Roles in Domiciliary Service: The Kent Community Care Project," *Gerontologist*, 20 (June 1980), 288–99.

12. *Federal Register*, 45 (March 21, 1980), 18885.

13. Peter F. Drucker, "On Managing the Public Service Institution," *Public Interest*, 33 (Fall 1973), 46.

14. Yeheskel Hasenfeld, *Human Service Organizations* (Englewood Cliffs: Prentice-Hall, 1982), chap. 8.

15. Charlane Brown and Mary O'Day, "Services to the Elderly," in *Handbook of the Social Services*, ed. Gilbert and Specht.

16. When efficiency is substituted for effectiveness as the basic measure of program performance the quality of service declines. As Lipsky points out, "there are many ways to save money by eroding the quality of service without appearing to do so. They include offering services on a group rather than individual basis, substituting paraprofessionals . . . for regular staff, and conversely, forcing professionals to handle clerical and other routine chores, reducing the time they have to interact with their clients" (Michael Lipsky, *Street-level Bureaucracy* [New York: Russell Sage Foundation, 1980], p. 171).

17. Ronald Randall, "Presidential Power versus Bureaucratic Intransigence: The Influence of the Nixon Administration on Welfare Policy," *American Political Science Review*, 73 (Sept. 1979), 806.

18. See, for example, SRI International, *Using New Governance Tools to Solve Local Government Problems: A Program of Research into Emerging Nonservice Approaches to Social Welfare and Community Development Problems* (Menlo Park, Calif.: SRI International Publications, Jan. 1979), and Carol Whitecomb and Maryann Miskiewicz, "Tapping New Resources," *Public Welfare*, 40 (Winter 1982), 16–22.

19. David Winston, "The Department of Health and Human Services," *Mandate for Leadership*, ed. Charles Heatherly (Washington, D.C.: Heritage Foundation, 1981), p. 252.

20. SRI International, *New Governance Tools*; Whitecomb and Miskiewicz, "Tapping New Resources."

21. Statement of Ken Scholen, Director, Home Equity Conversion Project, Madison, Wisconsin, to U.S. House of Representatives Select Committee on Aging, Subcommittee on Housing and Consumer Interests, July 29, 1981 (mimeographed).

22. For a cogent analysis of how these plans may interact with established income maintenance programs, see Susan Blumenstein and Gale M. Harmann, "The Effect of Reverse Annuity Mortgages on SSI." *U.C. Davis Law Review*, 16 (1983), 435–61.

23. See, for example, R. F. Conner, "Toward a Consumer Evaluation of Government Services," *Contemporary Psychology*, 21: 3 (1976), 179–80; R. H. Hessler and M. J. Walters, "Consumer Evaluation Research: Indications for Methodology, Social Policy and the Role of the Sociologist," *Sociological Quarterly*, 17 (Winter 1976), 74–89; and Mady Helme Kimmich, "The Emerging Role of Consumer Preference in the Measurement of Service Quality," University of California, Berkeley, School of Social Welfare (mimeo, n.d.).

24. Kenneth Webb and Harry Hatry, *Obtaining Citizen Feedback: The Application of Citizen Surveys to Local Governments* (Washington, D.C.: Urban Institute Press, 1973).

25. Brian Stipak, "Citizens' Satisfaction with Urban Services: Potential Misuse as a Performance Indicator," *Public Administration Review*, 39 (Jan./Feb. 1979), 46–52; Neil Gilbert and Joseph Eaton, "Who Speaks for the Poor," *Journal of the American Institute of Planners*, 36 (Nov. 1970), 411–16; George L. Kelling, Jony Pate, Duane Dieckman, and Charles Brown, "The Kansas City Preventive Patrol Experiment: A Summary Report," in Gene V. Glass, ed., *Evaluation Studies Review Annual* (Beverly Hills: Sage, 1976), vol. 1, pp. 631–37.

26. Mary Ann Scheirer, "Program Participants' Positive Perceptions: Psychological Conflict of Interest in Social Program Evaluation," in Lee Sechrest et al., eds., *Evaluation Studies Review Annual* (Beverly Hills: Sage, 1979), vol. 4, pp. 407–24; Malcolm Bush and Andrew Gordon, "The Advantages of Client Involvement," in Thomas Cook et al., eds., *Evaluation Studies Review Annual* (Beverly Hills: Sage, 1978), vol. 3, pp. 767–83.

27. Scheirer, *Participants' Perceptions*; Donald Campbell, "Reforms as Experiments," in F. G. Caro, ed., *Readings in Evaluation Research* (New York: Russell Sage, 1977), pp. 172–204.

28. Milton Friedman, "The Role of Government in Education," *Economics and the Public Interest*, ed. Robert A. Solo (New Brunswick, N.J.: Rutgers University Press, 1955).

29. Christopher Jencks et al., *Education Vouchers: A Report on Financing Elementary Education by Grants to Parents* (Cambridge, Mass.: Center for the Study of Public Policy, 1970).

30. For analyses of this resistance to the voucher demonstration see David Cohen and Eleanor Farrar, "Power to Parents? The Story of Education Vouchers," *Public Interest*, 48 (Summer 1977), 72–97, and E. G. West, "Choice or Monopoly in Education," *Policy Review*, 15 (Winter 1981), 103–17.

31. Paul Wortman and Robert St. Pierre, "The Educational Voucher Demonstration: A Secondary Analysis," *Education and Urban Society*, 9 (Aug. 1977), 471–91; Cohen and Farrar, "Power to Parents?"

32. Cohen and Farrar, "Power to Parents?"

33. Milton Friedman and Rose Friedman, *Free to Choose* (New York: Avon, 1979), pp. 162–63.

34. P. Barker, "Preliminary Analysis of Metropolitan Achievement Test Scores, Voucher and Title 1 Schools, 1972–73," in D. Weiler, ed., *A Public School Voucher Demonstration: The First Year at Alum Rock, Technical Appendix* (Santa Monica, Calif.: Rand Corporation, 1974), pp. 120–30, Technical Report R-1495/2.

35. R. Klitgaard, "Preliminary Analysis of Achievement Test Scores in Alum Rock Voucher and Nonvoucher Schools, 1972–73," in Weiler, ed., *Voucher Demonstration*, pp. 105–19.

36. Wortman and St. Pierre, "Educational Voucher Demonstration."

37. R. Crain, *Analysis of Achievement Test Outcomes in the Alum Rock Voucher Demonstration, 1974–75* (Santa Monica, Calif.: Rand Corporation, 1976), Technical Report WN-9593-NIE.

38. For the details of the experiment see Marc Bendick, Jr., and Anne O. Squire, "The Three Experiments," *Housing Vouchers for the Poor*, ed. Raymond J. Struyk and Marc Bendick, Jr. (Washington, D.C.: Urban Institute Press, 1981), pp. 51–75.

39. Raymond J. Struyk, "Policy Questions and Experimental Responses," in ibid., p. 13.

40. Francis J. Cronin, "Consumption Responses to Constrained Programs," in ibid., p. 129–57.

41. Friedman and Friedman, *Free to Choose*, p. 110.

42. For a review of various negative income tax schemes see James C. Vadakin, "A Critique of the Guaranteed Annual Income," *Public Interest*, 11 (Spring 1968), 53–66. See also Nancy Duff Levy and Michael Trister's "Status of Welfare Reform: Enactment Likely by Early 1972," *Clearinghouse Review*, 5 (Jan. 1972), 1–3. Levy and Trister's optimism proved unwarranted; for some of the reasons see Daniel P. Moynihan, *The Politics of a Guaranteed Income: The Nixon Administration and the Family Assistance Plan* (New York: Random House, 1973).

43. Michael Keeley et al., "The Labor-Supply Effects and Costs of Alternative Negative Income Tax Programs," *Journal of Human Resources*, 13: 6 (Winter 1978), 3–26.

44. Martin Anderson, *Welfare; The Political Economy of Welfare Reform* (Stanford, Calif.: Hoover Institution Press, 1978), pp. 104–27.

45. For details see John E. Coons and Stephen D. Sugarman, *Education by Choice: The Case for Family Control* (Berkeley: University of California Press, 1978).

46. West, "Choice or Monopoly," p. 116, notes that public opinion polls revealed that if Coons and Sugarman's proposal had qualified for the ballot in 1980, it would have been a close vote.

PART II

THE PLIGHT OF
UNIVERSAL SOCIAL SERVICES

THREE

THE DRIFT TOWARD UNIVERSALISM

From the early 1960s through 1980 there was a quiet revolution in the welfare state. While the brawly rhetoric of the War on Poverty and related federal reform initiatives of the 1960s encouraged the poor and minorities to wrestle for increased political power and a larger share of community resources, another form of redistribution was taking place, almost unnoticed. This redistribution was based on changing eligibility standards in federal legislation that provided the middle class with access to social welfare services traditionally reserved for the poor.

In the United States up through the 1960s, access to the public social services was not a cause to stir the hearts and minds of the middle class. Interestingly, the situation in most modern industrialized countries is very different. In Britain, for example, middle-class access to public social services has long been a fundamental issue of national social policy. The Beveridge Report of 1942, which set the framework for Britain's modern welfare state, endorsed the principle that health and welfare services be made available to all citizens as a social right. Although this principle has yet to be fully realized, universal entitlement to public social services receives a good deal of political support, especially from Britain's Labour party. The Conservative party is, naturally, of a different persuasion, preferring the selective approach to entitlement, whereby eligibility for public social services is determined by a means test under which only the poor may qualify.

In the ideological debates between universalists and selectivists, those who favor the universal approach emphasize the preservation of dignity and the enhancement of social solidarity that obtain when society is not divided into clear-cut groups of givers and receivers. According to this view entitlement to social services depends not upon being rich or poor, brilliant or dull, healthy or ill, but derives from the badge of citizenship to which all members of society may claim an equal right. The essence of universalist sentiment is captured by a brief exchange between Julian West and Dr. Leete, protagonists in Edward Bellamy's classic socialist Utopian vision, *Looking Backward*. West inquires about the criteria for dividing the national wealth among the citizenry: "By what title does the individual claim his particular share?" West asks. "What is the basis of his allotment?" "His title," replies Dr. Leete, "is his humanity. The basis of his claim is the fact that he is a man."[1]

However, those who prefer the selectivist approach to social service allocation have persuasive arguments too, especially in practical matters of finance. Selectivists are quick to calculate the immediate and significant tax savings that accrue to the community when free public social services are offered only to those who could not otherwise afford them. While there is much validity to these claims of immediate savings, the calculations are not always so conclusive as they may seem. As Richard Titmuss noted, when access to services requires a means test that is demeaning, time consuming, or otherwise inconvenient, those in need are often discouraged from applying until their problems reach critical proportions; intervention at that advanced state of ailment is difficult and usually more expensive than early treatment, particularly for health-related problems.[2] Hence, for certain problems the universal approach, which encourages "an ounce of prevention" through early service utilization, may be more economical in the long run than the determination of eligibility according to selective procedures, which can inhibit early access to service. It is also argued that universal programs are less expensive to administer than selective service allocations, which require repeated screening to ensure that recipients continue to be eligible. In the final tally, though, it must be conceded that the selective approach is still more economical than universal coverage for most social services.

When the debate shifts from costs to benefits, selectivists cannot lay strong claim to some of the humanistic results such as preservation of client dignity and enhancement of social solidarity that are attributed to universalism. Instead they observe that, by restricting social service benefits to the poor, the selective approach effects a greater and more equitable redistribution of community resources than would occur under universal coverage. There are many other social issues, questions of value and fact, conflicting principles, and occasionally moral admonishments that enliven the universal/selective debates.[3] The point here is that for all their philosophical spark and social significance, British debates on the merits of universal versus selective approaches to eligibility for social welfare services have not attracted much of an audience in this country.

Although social welfare in the United States inherited many basic precepts from the British system, the notion of universal access to social services did not develop a strong political foothold on these shores. From the "friendly visiting" in the charity organization movement of the 1880s to the 1962 "service" amendments of the Social Security Act, social services in the United States had been seen fundamentally as measures to sustain and rehabilitate the poor. Underlying this view is the assumption that to be poor is indicative of some personal defect that social casework services might correct. On that belief the friendly visitors went forth to strike at the moral roots of poverty. They sought to uplift the character and ambitions of the poor by providing ethical guidance, practical advice, and personal models of the virtues and rewards of decent middle-class behavior.

Up through the first half of the twentieth century in one form or another social services in the United States concentrated on correcting the personal defects of the poor. This objective was prominently expressed in the 1962 amendments to the Social Security Act, which made funds available for states to provide intensive social casework services aimed at preventing and reducing economic dependency. The focus here was on eliminating poverty rather than providing a network of care and supportive services that might improve the general quality of life. These so-called service amendments were designed for people on public assistance and mainly offered provisions for psychological analysis and restoration. As it turned out, these services were not distinguished for their success in reducing economic dependency. On the contrary, the dramatic increase of almost 1 million recipients added to public assistance rolls between 1962 and 1966 must have led a few legislators to wonder whether the new services did not in some way contribute to the problem they were supposed to solve.

Undoubtedly, the association of social services with the poor and notions of personal defect have had a restraining effect on middle-class enthusiasm for these services. In the United States most people have perceived the recipients of public social services as being faintly disreputable. This perception helps to explain why until recently there have been few demands, even fewer concessions, and relatively little political debate over extending public social services to the middle class. By the mid-1960s, however, the doors to an array of public social services began opening to a middle-class clientele. At the same time, that clientele became more favorably disposed toward utilization of these services. Before we pursue the reasons underlying this development, let us first examine some of the concrete legislative actions that have paved the way.

EXPANDING ENTITLEMENT

From 1962 to 1980 there were a consistent loosening of social service eligibility standards and a concomitant broadening in the client base of the welfare state. While the impetus for this movement is related to several federal programs, the drift toward universalism is best exemplified in legislative trends leading up to the Title XX amendments of the Social Security Act.

Any discussion of the unfolding of social services under the Social Security Act must take cognizance of the tremendous increase in federal spending that occurred in this area during the decade from 1963 to 1973. Between 1963 and 1971 federal grants to states for social services grew more than three-fold, from approximately $194 million to $740 million. This was a moderate rate of growth compared to the precipitous rise from $740 million to $1.7 billion that occurred between 1971 and 1972. While $1.7 billion was no trifling sum, when state estimates for 1973 indicated a potential increase to $4.7 billion, Congress was prompted to enact a $2.5-billion ceiling on federal expenditures for social services, which held through 1979.

This unprecedented rise in federal social service grants had less to do with the overall expansion of services offered, though some expansion did take place, than with the transfer of local social service costs from states to the federal government. The elasticity of the 1967 social service amendments to the Social Security Act coupled with permissive attitudes of federal officials had allowed federal social service funds to be used for the fiscal relief of the states. How all this came about is a fascinating chapter in the evolution of public social services which Martha Derthick illuminates with lucid detail in her *Uncontrollable Spending for Social Service Grants.*[4]

Although it is important to appreciate the explosive growth of federal funding as a force in the general development of social services, our concern here is with the changing structure of eligibility for services that accompanied the expanded base of federal support. The rise in federal expenditures can be seen, perhaps, as a quantitative measure of the qualitative transformation of eligibility standards, which can be traced from the 1962 service amendments to the Title XX amendments of 1974.

Under the 1962 Social Security Amendments, those eligible for social services included people receiving public assistance as well as former recipients and others who, in light of their precarious life circumstances, were judged likely to request public assistance in the near future. The *near future* was administratively defined as within one year of their request for services. Although these eligibility standards extended the possibility of service delivery beyond the immediate public assistance population, in practice this possibility was not realized. At that early stage, both program funds and trained social service workers were in relatively short supply. As political support for the 1962 amendments was predicated on the idea that intensive social service could reduce the size of public assistance rolls, the recipient population clearly held first priority on service allocations. Despite these immediate limitations, the future direction for extending service eligibility was established in principle.

The realization of this principle followed shortly, as the 1962 eligibility criteria were extended in two directions by the Social Security Amendments of 1967. Under these amendments persons became eligible for social services if they were considered to be potential welfare recipients within the next five years, rather than one year as previously stipulated. Even more significant, the concept of *group eligibility* was introduced, a concept whereby residents of low-income neighborhoods and other groups that could be defined as containing a high proportion of poverty-stricken members, such as those in institutional settings, became eligible for service.

By 1972 nonwelfare recipients were well represented among the social service clientele and growing in number. As previously noted, one reason for this development is that the 1967 amendments had provided a loophole through which the states began to squeeze many nonwelfare recipients of locally funded services into federally funded programs that reimbursed 75% of costs to the states. Congressional efforts to stem the tide of universal access to services (and more important, the costs of this access) were reflected in the Revenue Sharing Act of 1972, which placed a $2.5-billion cap on social service expenditures. At the same time a 90/10 restriction was devised, which required that 90% of service expenditures go directly to clients on public assistance. The legislation contained other measures and guidelines that seemed to reflect growing resistance to the drift toward universalism. While the $2.5-billion ceiling held, implementation of the 90/10 rule was postponed and never went into effect. Instead, efforts to contain the drift toward universalism were abandoned with the passage of the Title XX amendments of the Social Security Act in 1974.[5]

With an initial budget of $2.5 billion, the Title XX program provided the largest single source of federal funding for social services in the United States. This figure, however, did not represent "new" funds; Title XX incorporated the social service provisions originally financed under categorical programs in Titles I (Old Age Assistance), IV-A (Aid to Families with Dependent Children), X (Aid to the Blind), and XIV (Aid to the Permanently and Totally Disabled) of the Social Security Act. What was new and different about Title XX was the straight population-based formula on which these funds were to be allocated among the states, the high degree of discretion allowed to states in deciding how these monies were to be used within their jurisdictions, and the revised eligibility criteria that further extended social service entitlements to the middle class.

Under Title XX three basic categories of recipients were originally defined: income maintenance, income eligible, and universal.

People in the *income maintenance* category are those receiving public assistance, supplemental security income, or Medicaid; they are poor according to the means-tested standards that income maintenance applicants must satisfy to receive financial aid. The Title XX guidelines required that at least 50% of service expenditures in each state be directed to people in this category.[6] This allows considerably more latitude for service delivery to the nonpoor than the 90/10 rule endorsed in the 1972 Revenue Sharing Act.

Income eligible recipients include people who earn up to 115% of their state's median income, which for 1981 amounted to between $21,000 to $28,000 in most states. Within this group the states may offer services free-of-charge to those whose income does not exceed 80% of the state median, which is between $14,500 and $19,500 in most states. For people earning in the range of 80 to 115% of the state's median income, Title XX services are not provided free of charge. But they may be offered on a subsidized basis for reasonable income-related fees.

Recipients in the *universal* category receive a group of services which states may provide to all citizens without regard to income; such services consist of information and referral, protective services for children and adults, and family planning services.

The states have a degree of flexibility in the application of these eligibility guidelines to the social services that they offer under the Title XX program. In the first quarter of implementation, from October to December 1975, there were approximately 2.4 million Title XX service recipients throughout the country. More than ½ million of those recipients were in the new category of "income eligibles." (Despite the fact that in 1975 eligibility criteria for this group often amounted to earnings of between $16,000 and $19,000, they were curiously referred to as the "working poor" in the first federal report on Title XX implementation.) More than ¼ million recipients were in the universal category.[7] Thus, from the outset approximately 32% of the Title XX service recipients were not required to qualify for services under the strict means-tested eligibility criteria associated with public assistance programs. We must recognize that these figures do not represent the actual quantity or quality of services that were rendered to different groups. For example, the Comprehensive Annual Service Plan for Arizona indicates that 52% of all individuals to be served by the Title XX programs would be eligible under universal standards. However, the estimated costs of services to that group were only 12% of the total for all Title XX programs.[8] This reflects the fact that large numbers of nonpoor clients are eligible for inexpensive and short-term information and referral services.

During the first year of Title XX, the planning process and public response were of necessity a hurried affair. Awareness of the new possibilities for middle-class access to social services was still slight.

As the public perceptions of these possibilities sharpened, pressure for middle-class entitlements increased. In Missouri, for example, the public response to the state's first Title XX plan included recommendations to expand eligibility for services from those at 80% of the median income, which was the maximum eligibility level set at the state's option, to 115% of the median income, which is the maximum level permitted under federal guidelines.[9] And in California the planned parenthood agencies launched a campaign to have family planning services for teenagers classified as a universal service under Title XX.

By September 1977, the last quarter of the second Title XX year, the number of recipients had grown to 3.5 million people. More importantly within this group the proportion who qualified for service under the "income eligible" and "universal" categories had gone from 32% in 1975 to 45% in 1977.[10] The currents of universalism continued to gain momentum in 1978 with the addition of a fourth category for determining access to Title XX services, known as "group eligibility." This is a flexible arrangement that allows states to designate groups of people with similar characteristics or living in specified geographical areas as eligible for service without recourse to individual means tests. The only limiting condition is that, however the groups are defined, states must be able to demonstrate that at least 75% of the group members have incomes of no more than 90% of the state's median income, adjusted for family size.

Theoretically, by carefully designing the requisite groups, one could allocate almost the entire population of each state to one group or another in which three-quarters of the individuals have incomes of less than 90% of the state's median income; single parents, the elderly, certain minorities, veterans, residents of certain census tracts, and alcoholics, for instance, could collectively embrace a substantial segment. While this form of social gerrymandering would go somewhat beyond the spirit of group-eligibility regulations, its possibility suggests how far the letter of the law might tolerate extending universal coverage. By 1979 more than half the states were utilizing some form of group eligibility.

To claim that, overnight, the Title XX amendments opened universal access to social services in the United States would be an exaggeration. That they wrought a pronounced trend in this direction is evident when we compare the relaxed standards of entitlement to social services currently operating to the stringent means tests for public assistance that governed eligibility for these services in 1962.

UNIVERSAL PROVISIONS: WHO GETS SERVED?

In contrast to the various eligibility regulations governing the Title XX provisions, services under the Older Americans Act of 1965 have been available on a universal basis since this program's inception. From an initial appropriation of $7.5 million in 1966, the Older Americans Act rapidly matured into an operation of approximately $699 million by 1978. In 1972, Title VII was added to the act authorizing the provision of nutrition services. The 1973 amendments to the act established a network of more than 600 Area Agencies on Aging, charged with developing comprehensive social service systems for the elderly in the regions under their jurisdiction. The array of services they fund include counseling and mental health, homemaker/ chore, housing repair, information and referral, transportation, education and employment, legal aid, and recreational activities.

While the Older Americans Act supports research, training, and volunteer programs, the major portion of its appropriations is devoted to the provision of social services. Between 1975 and 1978 appropriations for nutrition and Title III planning and services almost doubled from $207 to $403 million.[11] Eligibility for these social services extends to all persons sixty years and older without regard to their income or assets. The retired executive in his condominium and the widowed housekeeper in a transient hotel room are equally entitled to phone one of the many dial-a-ride systems for the elderly, have a vehicle provide door-to-door service to the nearest nutrition center, enjoy a meal and the company of other elders there, and then be given a ride home virtually free of charge. In 1979 there were approximately 3,000 transportation projects and more than 6,600 nutrition programs (delivering more than a quarter-of-a-million meals daily) serving the elderly.[12]

Although the incidence of poverty among the elderly tends to be higher than in the population as a whole, most of the elderly are not poor. Estimates of the percentage of older persons in poverty range from a low of 5 to a high of 25% "at or near the poverty level," with the U.S. Census Bureau landing in the middle on a figure of 15.3% in

1975.[13] Assuming that the census data provide the most accurate estimate, well over 80 percent of the elderly currently eligible for the comprehensive array of social services supported by the Older Americans Act have incomes above the poverty level.

The fact that the elderly who are not poor may be eligible for services is no assurance, of course, that they will participate. But when access to social services is governed by universal criteria, program officials are most concerned about securing the participation of clients at the lower end of the socioeconomic scale; those in the higher ranges usually take advantage of social entitlements without much prodding. In line with this concern, the regulations implementing the Older Americans Comprehensive Service Amendments of 1973 required that, where possible, low-income and minority elderly be served at least in proportion to their number in the community. Evidence from a 1975 study by the General Accounting Office suggests that many of the Area Agencies on Aging had a difficult time meeting this minimal requirement for the proportional distribution of services.[14] The middle-class elderly, it seems, are among the major beneficiaries of the universal orientation to service in the Older Americans Act.

A similar result is apparent in the allocation of social provisions under the Community Mental Health Centers Act of 1963 as amended, which by 1980 was supporting a national system of more than 600 centers, each serving catchment areas of 75,000 to 200,000 people. As conceived in the 1963 legislation and its amendments, the Community Mental Health Centers Act was intended to make a range of professional mental health services available to all catchment area residents without regard to income. Within this universal framework, program officials were eager to ensure that these services would reach the poor and the most severely disturbed clients. Accordingly, states were instructed to formulate plans that assigned funding priorities to catchment areas based on the prevalence of chronic unemployment, low-income families, substandard housing, and mental illness; additionally, federal regulations proclaimed that centers should "furnish below cost or without charge a reasonable volume of service to persons unable to pay."[15]

Despite these directives the community mental health centers did not gravitate much toward poverty areas. In the implementation of state plans priorities were often reversed.[16] It was more a matter of economics than bad faith. Poor areas could demonstrate need, a derivative of which was their frequent inability to generate the matching funds to qualify for construction and staffing grants. The "reasonable volume of services" stipulation was the kind of regulatory sieve designed to advance good intentions without the filaments to screen for compliance.

To amplify the delivery of services to the poor, the 1970 amendments to the Community Mental Health Centers Act increased the level and duration of funding for centers in poverty areas. Nevertheless, between 1970 and 1972 there were few new centers funded in poverty areas.[17] Then the revised regulations issued in 1972 hit upon an alternative solution. Poverty was redefined. Under these new regulations, 25% of the catchment areas in each state were automatically classified as poverty areas, based on the ordering of average family incomes of the areas within each state. (While 25% of the population residing in designated "poverty areas" on first glance may seem a somewhat inflated estimate, these calculations are downright restrained compared to the measures used by the Economic Development Administration, which place 84.5% of the population in "distressed areas" eligible for federal assistance under the Public Works and Redevelopment Act.)[18]

These liberal adjustments in the definition of poverty areas did not have much effect on the clientele or types of problems brought to community mental health centers. An examination of the populations served by the centers reveals a decreasing emphasis on the chronically or severely mentally ill. In 1975 only 10% of the 699,709 unduplicated cases served by community mental health centers were diagnosed as schizophrenic, a drop from 19% in 1970; in contrast, the proportion of cases classified as "social maladjustment," "no mental disorders," or "deferred diagnosis and non-specific conditions" rose from 4.6% in 1970 to 21.8% in 1975.[19] Adding cases classified as "neuroses and personality disorders" to these categories brings the treatment of milder types of mental health problems up to 43% of the 1975 community mental health centers' caseload.[20]

Other data and a more upbeat interpretation of the facts, cited by a National Institute of Mental Health official, indicate that in 1972 one-third of the 846,336 cases served by the centers were diagnosed as psychotic and 53% of these clients came from families with less than $5,000 income.[21] Counting and diagnostic classification in a field as vast and ephemeral as community mental health are often imprecise and open to dispute. (It appears that the exact number of operating centers is difficult even for the National Institute on Mental Health to pin down. One major study reports that over the entire two-year period of investigation "not once did different Institute officials agree on their estimates of the number of operating or funded centers.")[22]

Yet, whatever the exact diagnostic breakdown, number of cases served, and the percentage of poor people in the community mental health client population, no one disputes that middle-class recipients of subsidized services are highly represented in this group.

WHY MIDDLE-CLASS ENTITLEMENTS?

What accounts for the increasing number of middle-class people who have become eligible for social services since 1960? Among the reasons that might explain this trend is the growing realization that middle-class people enjoy no special immunity from the contingencies of life in modern industrialized society. Unemployment, drug abuse, divorce, age-related impairments, and mental illness are distributed throughout the socioeconomic classes in society. The poor undoubtedly have more than their share but they hold no monopoly on human frailties and suffering. They are more vulnerable to the vagaries of the economic system and also are accustomed to existence on the economic margins of society.

During the early 1960s there was great ferment surrounding the discovery of poverty in America and the needs of the poor. Michael Harrington's *The Other America* was a grim account of the conditions and magnitude of poverty in this country.[23] This work apparently helped crystallize President Kennedy's determination to initiate an antipoverty program in 1963.[24] The War on Poverty was legislated a year later under Lyndon Johnson. On the academic front Harrington's work inspired a surge of research on the characteristics and effects of poverty. The outpouring of literature in the following four years included six major anthologies: two under the title of "Poverty in America," two examining "Poverty in (Amid) Affluence," one declaring "Poverty as a Public Issue," and one offering "New Perspectives on Poverty."

By the mid-1970s public concern about the prevalence and consequences of poverty had diminished. Official census figures showed that the rate of poverty had declined almost 50% (from 22.4 to 12% of the population) between 1959 and 1975. Going beyond the basic income reported in the census data, a number of studies were beginning to suggest that poverty in the United States was, if not already extinct, well under control and headed in that direction. Along with the basic measures of income, these studies appraised the array of in-kind benefits such as food stamps, public housing, Medicaid, child care, and transportation services that had multiplied since the 1960s. A study of welfare recipients in New York City by the Rand Corporation revealed that, by counting cash and the dollar value of in-kind benefits, the average four-person AFDC case received $6,590 in 1974.[25] That sum was well above the 1974 poverty threshold of $5,038 for a nonfarm family of four persons. On the national level, estimates by the Congressional Budget Office found that, by including in-kind assistance, only 6.9% of the population was below the poverty level in 1977, which was almost half the official figure of 12% that emerged when the value of in-kind benefits was not included.[26] Based on these estimates, the war on poverty had been won, according to Martin Anderson, "except for perhaps a few mopping-up operations."[27] Anderson's view is more optimistic than popular opinion (and antagonistic to liberal sentiments), but it captured a perception that was gaining tacit acceptance. In the late 1970s poverty was a fading issue in government circles.

With poverty on the wane as a public issue the spotlight of public concern had shifted. It was the middle class whose needs pressed for attention in the 1970s. Tom Wolfe dubbed this era the "me decade."[28] Individual thirst for self-fulfillment seemed to deepen almost in proportion to a diminishing interest in communal well-being. Public sympathy for the indigent dissolved as many middle-class people were beginning to feel somehow deprived and in need of government relief. Everyone was considered a rival, as Christopher Lasch put it, "for the favors conferred by a paternalistic state."[29] This spirit of the times was reflected in the growing demand for food stamps among undergraduates—braving the temporary, often self-styled, "poverty" of middle-class student life that was virtually de rigueur at the elite universities. In one stroke, eligibility for food stamps granted formal recognition of the college students' "poverty status" and alleviated some of the pinch of this condition.

Connections between the self-centered zeitgeist of the 1970s and increasing middle-class entitlements to social services suggest a speculative line of thought that identifies the cultural context but not the propelling forces of change. Moving from the spirit of the era to more concrete observations we can detect certain empirical trends in employment, family life, and the elderly population that have heightened middle-class claims to social services.

The first trend concerns the growing participation of women in the labor force. Whether out of economic necessity or social liberation (an odd choice that forms a paradox of modern times) between 1960 and 1979 the proportion of married women in the labor force with children under six years of age more than doubled from 18 to 43%; for those with children aged 6–17 participation rates climbed from 39 to 59%. Most of these married women worked full time.

These data signify, on the one hand, that women are assuming increasing financial responsibility for family well-being. On the other hand, they reflect diminishing time and effort devoted to child-rearing responsibilities. The desirability of this trend is not self-evident and many questions have been raised concerning its impact on the traditional values of family life. President Nixon vetoed the Child Development Act of 1974, which proposed a public network of child-care centers providing infant care, preschool programs, evening care, and the like, because in his words, "Good public policy requires that we enhance rather than diminish both parental authority and parental involvement with children, particularly in those decisive early years when social attitudes and a conscience are formed and religious and moral principles are first inculcated."[30] Government-sponsored day care, it was thought, would eventually undermine parental responsibilities. In contrast, those who endorse the expansion of public day care see these services as a potential "safety valve" or support system to help families cope with the changes and pressures of modern times.[31]

While debate over day care and family relations continues (see chap. 5 for a more detailed account), there is no arguing with the facts of an increasing number of working mothers and a growing demand for publicly sponsored child-care services. This demand is not from the poor alone. Day-care services are expensive. To provide an environment that nurtures emotional and intellectual development the American Academy of Pediatrics has recommended a ratio of one worker to every four children under three years of age; the Child Welfare League of America favors a one-to-two ratio. To maintain these and other standards for high-quality day-care facilities, annual cost estimates vary between $1,500 and $2,500 per child. Without public subsidy the price of quality day care is burdensome, even for the middle class.

The substantial demand for day-care provisions is revealed in the Title XX program, where over 20% of the annual expenditures have gone to finance these services. It is unclear exactly what proportion of these services goes to middle-class recipients. Some observers claim that day-care services go primarily to poor clients.[32] However, in 1977 almost one-half (47.5%) of the Title XX day-care funds were allocated to families in the "income eligible" category, which in most states include those earning between 70 and 115% of the state's median income.[33] With the pressure growing for universal day-care services, $200 million of Title XX money in 1980 was earmarked for these provisions. What is more, these federal funds were offered without any local matching requirements. Although Title XX undoubtedly has extended a measure of day-care benefits to the middle class, a program even more advantageous to this group was initiated under the 1976 amendments to the Internal Revenue Code. This program allowed a tax credit of up to $800 for in-home and out-of-home child-care expenses incurred by working parents.

In addition to the growing participation of married women in the labor force, family life also experienced an unprecedented level of instability. Divorce rates rose by 112% between 1965 and 1979, at which point there was almost one divorce for every two marriages. Aside from the emotional turmoil, an immediate consequence of divorce is to leave both parties in reduced economic circumstances. This downward mobility is rapid as family resources are divided virtually overnight to support two households. The division of resources is rarely equal and many partners slide into poverty or just short of the line. Even those who remain comfortable by middle-class standards usually experience a strong sense of relative deprivation and feel painfully poor—a response to which any family having gone from an annual budget of say $40,000 to a modest, but hardly poverty-stricken, $20,000 can well attest. High divorce rates have unsettled the economic security of middle-class families. Amid this heightened uncertainty, universal access to public social services holds the attraction of an alternate support system to subsidize housing, food, mental health services, child care, and other benefits that would help secure the middle-class standard of living.

The third trend that has stimulated middle-class entitlements to social services concerns the changing position of the elderly. Geographic separation of elderly parents from the households of their children spiraled between 1957 and 1975 as the proportion of persons 65 years of age and older living with their children declined by 50%.[34] During the same period the number of people aged 65 and over increased by almost 50%, from approximately 15 to 22 million. As a group the elderly constitute a potent political force containing 17% of the nation's eligible voters in a population bloc that spans social, class, and ethnic lines.

When the poor retire, they usually stay poor. When middle-class people retire, they face the prospects of living on reduced, fixed incomes and struggling to hold the line against inflation. Both groups experience heightened vulnerability to physical impairment, social isolation, and the vagaries of the economic system. Facing the contingencies of old age, the middle class joins the poor, not in economic deprivation, but in becoming part of a "population-at-risk." The self-consciousness of the elderly as an "at-risk" population has been rising since the 1960s, kindled by the Older Americans Act of 1965, which established the Administration on Aging in the Department of Health, Education and Welfare. This rising self-consciousness has been accompanied by political demands for recognition of the special problems of the elderly. In Pennsylvania, for example, under pressure from elderly constituents in 1978, the legislature removed the Office for the Aging from the State Department of Public Welfare and made it a separate department with cabinet level status. Massachusetts had created a similar arrangement in 1971. The increased political activities by the elderly have been attended by growing claims of universal entitlement to provisions such as congregate/home-delivered meals, companionship/reassurance services, homemaker/chore services, transportation, recreation, and adult day-care arrangements.

CHANGING SCOPE AND PURPOSES OF SOCIAL SERVICES

With the expansion of middle-class entitlements since 1960, the scope and purpose of public social services have enlarged. The spreading scope of social services is seen in the diverse activities that evolved under federal support from the landmark Social Security amendments of 1962 to the Title XX amendments of 1974. In the 1962 amendments the principal thrust of social services was the reduction of poverty. This was to be accomplished through intensive social casework services that were supposed to rehabilitate the poor—changing their behaviors in ways that would help them to become economically independent. Social services also included other basic forms of provision such as homemakers and foster home care. However, the essential feature of the 1962 amendments was the provision of social casework services. While this was not specified in the law, as Derthick points out, "Welfare professionals in the Bureau of Family Services knew more or less what they meant by 'services.' Fundamentally and at a minimum it meant casework by a trained social worker."[35]

There is an intangible quality about casework services that makes it difficult to specify the exact nature of the provision. This vagueness has led to the cynical observation that casework "is anything done for, with, or about the client by the social worker. If a social worker discusses a child's progress in school with an AFDC mother, a check is made under 'Services related to education. . . .' When the discussion turns to the absent father and possible reconciliation a check is made under 'Maintaining family and improving family functioning.'"[36] In a similar vein this type of service has been characterized as "little more than a relatively infrequent, pleasant chat."[37] At its best, social casework is certainly a more skillful and nurturing enterprise than these comments depict. However, large caseloads, demands of eligibility certification (while trying to establish a casework relationship), diversity of clientele (many of whom did not need or want casework services but had to accept them), qualifications of staff (many of whom were not professionally trained), and omnipresent bureaucratic regulations of public assistance work were hardly conducive to the performance of social casework at its best. In any event, whatever its powers and benefits, casework was not a cure for poverty. The addition of almost 1 million recipients to the public assistance rolls between 1962 and 1966 testified unequivocally to this point.

Their failure to reduce economic dependency and their intangible quality combined to make social casework services a prime target of congressional disillusionment with public assistance. This was reflected in the 1967 Social Security amendments, in which casework services were no longer so prominent as they had been in 1962, when federal grants for social service went mainly to pay the salaries of caseworkers.[38] The 1967 amendments opened the way for a broader conception of social services that might qualify for federal support than those previously funded. Indeed, the regulations to implement the 1967 amendments contained such a comprehensive definition of social services that, Rein concludes, "literally almost any service was federally reimbursable."[39]

As federal support enveloped an increasing range of social service activities, greater emphasis came to be placed on the delivery of services that were more tangible than social casework. Federal officials began to draw the distinction between "soft" and "hard" services. According to Derthick, "advice and counselling from a caseworker were 'soft' in this managerial parlance and presumably less valuable than day-care centers or drug treatment centers, or work training, which were 'hard' and which were much more widely available in 1969 than in 1962 because of the intervening growth of public programs for social purposes."[40]

With the passage of the Title XX amendments in 1974 the movement toward diversification of federally financed social services reached new heights. Under Title XX each state could provide whatever social services were deemed appropriate for its communities. The only requirement was that these services be directed to one of five goals, which were so broadly formulated as to encompass virtually any scheme for service the imagination of social welfare planners could devise.

In the first year of implementation, plans for the 50 states and the District of Columbia specified a total of 1,313 services. Imposing some order on this array of provisions, federal planners grouped the services with common characteristics into 40 general categories for purposes of tabulation and analysis.[41] While not all these categories yield sharp distinctions between the most tangible and least tangible services, the data suggest that the emphasis on delivery of "hard" services which developed in the late 1960s continued to influence the emerging content of the social services under Title XX. For example, in the allocation of federal funds among all categories of service, child day care and homemaker services consistently come out on top of the list, accounting for approximately 33% of all Title XX expenditures.

Along with the increasing emphasis on tangible services and the diversification of service content a profound reorientation of purpose has taken place in the social services.[42] The services authorized by the 1962 amendments aimed primarily at the reduction of economic dependency and deprivation. Since then a broad-scope service network has evolved that is concerned to a large extent with provisions that go beyond meeting the basic needs of the poor. These provisions are directed more at enhancing human development and the general quality of life than at reducing poverty. Social services have embarked upon this broader mission in various program areas. For provisions under the Social Security Act, the first major step toward releasing service delivery from the nexus of economic dependency came in 1967, when income maintenance functions were administratively divorced from social services and moved to the Assistance Payments Administration. In 1977 this administrative separation at the federal level was concluded by placing all income maintenance programs under the Social Security Administration and joining the social service and human development programs under the Office of Human Development. The changing purpose that accompanied this administrative reorganization is reflected in the host of Title XX services (such as transportation, day care, homemaker-chore, and information and referral) not associated with notions of personal deficiency or lack of character that in the past marked the main provisions of social casework to those dependent on public aid.

The mission of promoting human development and improving the quality of life is similarly pursued in programs for the elderly and community mental health. The Older Americans Act supports diverse social, educational, and recreational programs to enrich the elderly's participation in community life. Considerable emphasis is also placed upon vehicles such as information and referral, transportation, and escort services that facilitate access to these programs and other resources. In 1977, for example, these provisions for the elderly's access to and wholesome engagement in community activities accounted for approximately 75% of the social service expenditures by Area Agencies on Aging.[43]

The Community Mental Health program did not spring from a broad mandate to nurture and advance the social/psychological well-being of the community. Originally it was inspired by President Kennedy's wish to create a community-based approach that would supplant state mental hospitals as the focal point for care and treatment of severely disturbed mental patients. The high cost, low rates of successful treatment, and frightful conditions in state mental hospitals lent weight to the general enthusiasm for the "bold, new approach" proposed in Kennedy's message to Congress in 1963.[44] However, as Community Mental Health Center client characteristics indicate, the objective of concentrating services upon the most severe mental health problems and impoverished groups was rapidly expanded to encompass middle-class clients and a large percentage of problems in such diagnostic categories as social maladjustment, neuroses, no mental disorder, deferred diagnosis, and nonspecific condition. Anxious, unhappy, and under stress, while often functioning at an adequate level, clients in these categories suffer from what Thomas Szasz calls "problems of living."[45] Mental health services provide emotional support, encouragement, and counseling to help these clients achieve a full and satisfactory life.

The developments in Community Mental Health, Older Americans Act, and Title XX programs illustrate a general trend in the evolution of social services in the American welfare state between 1960 and 1980. As the welfare state opened to middle-class recipients during this period, so too it enlarged the sphere of needs encompassed and the scope of services provided. With this movement toward universal entitlement the latitude of purpose spread from minimizing the insecurity and distress of poverty to the broader mission of promoting human development and the quality of life. In the course of changing the landscape of the welfare state, these events have brought to the surface some basic contradictions between the theory and consequences of universalism, which have contributed to the resurgence of selectivity that has emerged in the early 1980s.

NOTES

1. Edward Bellamy, *Looking Backward* (New York: Signet Classic, 1960; orig. publication, 1888), p. 75.

2. Richard M. Titmuss, *Essays on the Welfare State* (London: Unwin University Books, 1963), 2d ed., pp. 138–41.

3. For example, see Richard Titmuss, *Commitment to Welfare* (New York: Pantheon, 1968), pp. 113–23; Mike Reddin, "Universality versus Selectivity," *Political Quarterly*, 40 (Jan./Mar. 1969), 12–22; George Hoshino, "Britain's Debate on Universal or Selective Social Services," *Social Service Review*, 43 (Sept. 1969), 245–58; and Neil Gilbert and Harry Specht, *Dimensions of Social Welfare Policy* (Englewood Cliffs: Prentice-Hall, 1974), pp. 54–66.

4. Martha Derthick, *Uncontrollable Spending for Social Services Grants* (Washington, D.C.: Brookings Institution, 1975).

5. For a more detailed review of the developments leading up to Title XX, see Paul Mott, *Meeting Human Needs: The Social and Political History of Title XX* (Columbus, Ohio: National Conference on Social Welfare, 1976).

6. "Social Service Programs for Individuals and Families: Title XX of the Social Security Act," *Federal Register*, 40 (June 27, 1975), 40.

7. Social and Rehabilitation Service, DHEW, *Social Services U.S.A., Oct.-Dec., 1975* (Washington, D.C.: National Center of Social Statistics, 1975).

8. Arizona Department of Economic Security, *Final Comprehensive Annual Social Service Program Plan 1976* (Phoenix, Ariz.: Department of Economic Security, 1975).

9. Missouri Department of Social Services, *Final Comprehensive Annual Social Services Program Plan* (Jefferson City, Mo.: Dept. of Social Services, 1975), p. iii.

10. Social Security Administration, U.S. Department of Health and Human Services, "SSI Recipients and Title XX Services, July–September 1977," *Research and Statistics Note,* 14 (Dec. 17, 1980).

11. Carroll Estes, *The Aging Enterprise* (San Francisco: Jossey Bass, 1979), p. 51.

12. These figures are from Institute of Public Administration, *Improving Transportation Services for Older Americans: Volume I* (Washington, D.C.: Institute of Public Administration, Sept. 1980), and Kirschner Associates and Opinion Research Center, *Longitudinal Evaluation of the National Nutrition Program for the Elderly* (Washington, D.C.: U.S. Dept. of Health, Education and Welfare, Feb. 1979), OHDS no. 80-20240.

13. The low estimate comes from H. Watts and F. Skidmore, "An Update of the Poverty Picture," *Focus,* University of Wisconsin, Institute for Research on Poverty Newsletter, 1977; the high figure is offered in Estes, *Aging Enterprise*, p. 90; and the middle is shown in the U.S. Bureau of the Census, *Characteristics of the Population Below the Poverty Level,* Current Population Reports, ser. P-23, no. 59 (Washington, D.C.: Bureau of the Census, 1977).

14. U.S. General Accounting Office, *Local Area Agencies Help the Aging But Problems Need Correcting,* report by the Comptroller General of the United States (Washington, D.C., Aug. 2, 1977), p. 33.

15. Franklin Chu and Sharland Trotter, *The Madness Establishment* (New York: Grossman, 1974), pp. 86–104.

16. U.S. General Accounting Office, *The Community Mental Health Centers Pro-*

gram: Improvements Needed in Management, report by the Comptroller General of the United States (Washington, D.C., July 8, 1971).

17. Chu and Trotter, *Madness Establishment.*

18. Spencer Rich, *Washington Post* (May 4, 1980), cited in *Public Interest,* 60 (Summer 1980), 148.

19. Steven Segal, "Community Mental Health," in *Handbook of the Social Services,* ed. Neil Gilbert and Harry Specht (Englewood Cliffs: Prentice-Hall, 1981), pp. 186–87.

20. President's Commission on Mental Health, *Task Panel Reports, Vol. II* (Washington, D.C.: U.S. GPO, Feb. 15, 1978), p. 319.

21. Henry A. Foley, *Community Mental Health Legislation* (Lexington, Mass.: D.C. Heath, 1978), p. 127.

22. Chu and Trotter, *Madness Establishment,* p. 27.

23. Michael Harrington, *The Other America* (New York: Macmillan, 1962).

24. Arthur M. Schlesinger, Jr., *A Thousand Days* (Boston: Houghton Mifflin, 1965), p. 1010.

25. David W. Lyon, Philip Armstrong, James Hosek, and John McCall, *Multiple Welfare Benefits in New York City* (Santa Monica: Rand Corporation, 1976).

26. U.S. Congress, Congressional Budget Office, *Poverty Status of Families Under Alternative Definitions of Income* (Washington, D.C.: U.S. GPO, June 1977).

27. Martin Anderson, *Welfare: The Political Economy of Welfare Reform in the United States* (Stanford, Calif.: Hoover Institute Press, 1978), p. 37.

28. Tom Wolfe, "The 'Me' Decade and the Third Great Awakening," *New York Magazine,* Aug. 23, 1976, pp. 26–40.

29. Christopher Lasch, *The Culture of Narcissim* (New York: Warner Books, 1979), p. 22.

30. *New York Times,* Dec. 12, 1971, p. 4.

31. For a discussion of this issue see Carole Joffe, "Daycare Services," in *Handbook of the Social Services,* ed. Gilbert and Specht, pp. 63–65.

32. For example, see Gwen Morgan, *The Trouble With Title XX: A Review of Child Daycare Policy* (Washington, D.C.: Day Care and Child Development Council of America, 1977).

33. Social Security Administration, "SSI Recipients and Title XX Services."

34. Abraham Monk, "Family Supports in Old Age," *Social Work,* 24 (Nov. 1979), 537.

35. Derthick, *Uncontrollable Spending,* p. 9.

36. President's Commission on Income Maintenance, *Background Papers* (Washington, D.C.: U.S. GPO, 1970), p. 307.

37. Joel F. Handler and Jane Hollingsworth, *The Deserving Poor: A Study of Welfare Administration* (Chicago: Markham, 1971), p. 127.

38. Derthick, *Uncontrollable Spending,* p. 19.

39. Mildred Rein, "Social Services as a Work Strategy," *Social Service Review,* 49 (Dec. 1975), 519.

40. Derthick, *Uncontrollable Spending,* p. 19.

41. Social and Rehabilitation Service, DHEW, *Social Services.*

42. For a cogent analysis of this development see Rein, "Social Services."

43. Neil Gilbert, Harry Specht, Gary Nelson, and David Lindeman, *Services to the*

Elderly Under Title XX: An Analysis of National Trends, 1975–79 (Berkeley: Institute for Scientific Analysis, 1981).

44. President John F. Kennedy, "Message on Mental Illness and Mental Retardation," *Congressional Record,* 88th Cong., 1st sess., 1963, part 2, pp. 1744–49.

45. Thomas Szasz, *Myth of Mental Illness* (New York: Harper & Row, 1961).

FOUR

CONTRADICTIONS OF UNIVERSAL ENTITLEMENT

One of the most forceful claims for universal entitlement to social services is the social solidarity inspired by government's ministering to the common needs of all citizens irrespective of income. When everyone is eligible for subsidized services, even if fees are charged on a sliding scale, society is not sharply divided into classes of givers and receivers, and the latter are not stigmatized by recipient status. Universalism is believed thus to have a binding influence on the social fabric. The logic is sound, as far as this proposition is carried. The theoretical case for heightening social integration, however, fails in practice to take into account the inclinations of social service providers and client behavior. These inclinations and behaviors can be expressed in a few simple axioms of social service allocation:

For service providers:
Less troublesome clients will be served before more troublesome ones.
Those who can pay will be served before those who cannot.
Higher status clients will be served before lower status clients.

For clients:
Middle-class clients will obtain more knowledge about social service resources to meet their needs than lower-class clients.
When both middle-class and lower-class clients know where resources are available to meet their needs, the middle-class clients will be more effective in getting at the head of the line.

Some of these axioms reflect the fact that poor people are not so well versed as those from middle-class backgrounds in certain skills that facilitate access to social benefits. For example, one study estimates that approximately three-quarters of the heads of families in poverty possess at most an eighth grade reading-skill level. Yet, examining a range of social welfare programs in five states and the District of Columbia, this study found that 90% of the documents that clients are normally expected to read and fill out in applying to these programs required more than an eighth grade reading level; one-third of these documents required the reading skill of a person with some college education.[1] The greater physical mobility of middle-class applicants, who can more easily afford public and private transportation, also enhances their access to social welfare programs.

Implicit recognition of these middle-class advantages and efforts to compensate for them are evident in social welfare planners' attempts to guarantee low-income clients an adequate portion of social service allocations through measures such as: the Title XX requirement that 50% of expenditures go to those in the income maintenance category; the financial incentives to locate community mental health centers in poverty areas; and the mandate under the Older Americans Act that, where possible, low-income elderly be served in proportion to their number in the community. Even Richard Titmuss, the doyen of universalist thought, admits that fifteen years of experience with the universal, free-on-demand, provisions of Britain's National Health Service have shown that "the higher income groups know how to make better use of the Service; they tend to receive more specialist attention; they occupy more of the beds in better equipped and staffed hospitals; receive more elective surgery; have better maternity care; and are more likely to get psychiatric help and psychotherapy than low income groups."[2] Thus, although in theory universalism facilitates social integration of all classes, in practice the poor are often relegated to inferior services or wind up at the end of the line.

Universalist proposals typically begin with a humanistic philosophy of blending and integrating various income groups in an open system of services and end with all sorts of qualifications that try to ensure that the poor will receive some share of program benefits. A highly publicized report by the Carnegie Council on Children, for example, recommends universal entitlement to social services as the first principle for those "who care about the growth and development of this nation's children. This means services that are open to everyone—whatever race they are, whatever income they have, wherever they live, and whatever languages they speak." Qualifications to this firm statement begin immediately in the next paragraph with the condition that whenever services are in short supply "priority should be given to families where the well-being of the child and the integrity of the family are in greatest jeopardy for lack of services."

Further qualification by the end of that paragraph informs us that in practice "this will mean that priority will most often be given to families at the lower end of the income scale, to families *who cannot afford* to seek the service from private providers"[3] (emphasis added). At this point one might ask: Why should families that can afford to seek services from private providers be included in the first place if they are able to meet their needs without public intervention or subsidy?

One answer to this question returns to the theory of enhanced social solidarity. As already suggested, that theory does not correspond well in practice with the facts about disproportionate allocations of universal social services to middle-class beneficiaries. There is, however, a broader philosophical foundation for the advocacy of universal entitlement, which stems from beliefs about the proper degree and role of public intervention in society's economic affairs. The universalists' convictions about communal responsibility for individual well-being are compatible with a system in which most, if not all, of the economic affairs of society are conducted in the public sector.

In the United States individualism and the market economy, although not so unfettered as in the early days of capitalism, still hold the edge over socialist doctrine. While economic activity in the United States is heavily invested in the private sector, a system of welfare capitalism has developed in which social and economic markets coexist. Ideally, as suggested earlier, the economic market is impelled by individual initiative, ability, productivity, and the desire for profit. In contrast, the social market of the welfare state allocates benefits in response to need, dependency, charitable impulses, and the wish for communal security. There is an ambivalent relationship between the social and economic markets in industrialized capitalist societies. In part the relation is complementary in joining individual ambitions and collective responsibilities. In part the relation is antagonistic, reflecting competing ideologies seeking to extend their realms and protect their boundaries. It is in regard to the latter aspect of this relationship that universal social service entitlements form a wedge for driving public activity into areas in which private enterprise might otherwise be engaged.

From 1960 to 1980 efforts to extend the sphere of public activity in the United States under the mantle of universal social service entitlements have resulted not in strengthening the welfare state but in eroding its position. There are two reasons that the move toward universalism has undermined the American welfare state. First, the increasing proportion of middle-class clientele, drawn particularly from the elderly and families with working mothers, blurs the traditional distinction between consumers of social welfare services and consumers of services obtained on the economic market. Many of the services offered by the welfare state such as transportation, day care, homemaker/chore, meals, home repair, legal aid, and counseling have long been available for those who could afford to pay for them in the marketplace. Second, the growing emphasis on improving the quality of life that has accompanied the expanding client base of social services obscures the boundaries of purpose that separate the social and economic markets. To the extent that there is overlap in the consumer groups served by the social and economic markets and converging lines of purpose, the justification for a welfare state in a capitalist society is diminished.

This is not to suggest that the American welfare state is in jeopardy of being dismantled. It has, however, lost a considerable amount of political support from that enjoyed in the 1960s and 1970s, when the Great Society programs advanced the boundaries of the welfare state. In the wake of expanding welfare state activities a number of developments have modified the character of the social market. These developments, as noted in chapters 1 and 2, include an influx of profit-making agencies into the social market, a growing emphasis on consumer choice, a budding entrepreneurialism among social welfare professionals, and a drive for greater efficiency in social services through the application of cost–benefit accounting and other techniques of the economic market. As this movement toward the commercialization of the social market progresses, the welfare system emerging in the 1980s will be more influenced by capitalist doctrine than in any period since the era of industrial welfare in the first quarter of the twentieth century.

Herein lies, perhaps, the most lethal contradiction of universalism, briefly represented by the following cycle: Universal entitlement encourages expansion of social welfare services to the point of encompassing consumers and functions served by the economic market; when distinctions between the social and economic markets thus begin to fade, in a society strongly committed to the capitalist

doctrine, the preference for private enterprise over public intervention asserts itself; as a result private enterprise and capitalist doctrine
not only infiltrate the social market, but in so doing they engender
opposition to the communal goal of universal entitlement. In this
manner the indiscriminate cultivation of universal social services
sows the seeds of its own undoing.

Obviously, political and economic circumstances will influence
how and when this process comes to fruition. It is less likely to run
full cycle and generate effective political opposition to universal
social services in countries where socialist leanings are heavier than
in the United States. Even in capitalist systems, on the scale of political
feasibility it is always easier to extend new entitlements than to retract
those already awarded. And when cutbacks are made they are not
distributed evenly among all recipient groups; programs serving
politically well-organized groups usually fare somewhat better than
those without an active constituency. In these matters political philosophy is often tempered by economic opportunities and constraints.
Under conditions of steady economic growth universal social service
entitlements are more easily absorbed and encounter less resistance
than in periods of economic stagnation or declining growth. In the
American welfare state it appears that this process had come full cycle
by 1980. By that time, the movement toward universalism was beginning to ebb as changing economic and political conditions lent
impetus to the case for greater selectivity in the allocation of social
services.

RESURGENCE OF SELECTIVITY

Title XX, the Older Americans Act, and the Community Mental Health
Centers Act illustrate some of the most significant advances in
middle-class entitlements to social services made between 1960 and
1980. After the mid 1970s, however, we can detect some initial currents in opposition to the drift toward universalism. Between 1978
and 1979, for example, the maximum level of income used to determine eligibility for Title XX services increased in 6 states and decreased in 10 states (within the ceiling of 115% of the state's median
income established by federal regulations). Also by 1979 a growing
number of states had started to employ more stringent fee-for-service

policies, charging fees to recipients from families earning less than 80% of the median income of the state.[4]

In a similar vein, the 1978 amendments to the Older Americans Act required that preferences be given to providing services to older persons with the "greatest economic or social needs." "Social need" included "non-economic factors which restricted individual ability to carry out normal activities of daily living and which threatened an individual's capacity to live an independent life."[5] As the narrow definition of economic need pressed to circumscribe eligibility, the broad conception of social need held open the path of universal access. While the intent here was to increase the degree of selectivity, these regulations lacked the stringency needed to achieve more than a symbolic statement of purpose. Even the symbolic statement was diluted by the murky requirement of "preferences" for services to these categories, a common bureaucratic palliative for hard choices.

Universal services in the Community Mental Health Program temporarily experienced the shock of a hard choice in 1973, when the Nixon administration, seeking to phase out the program, impounded the federal funds appropriated for its support. Although these funds were later released by court order, opposition to the program continued. In 1974 President Ford vetoed a bill to extend the program. Overriding the Ford veto, Congress passed the 1975 amendments to the Community Mental Health Centers Act. These amendments provided the program's operating guidelines until the Mental Health Systems Act of 1980, which introduced a new series of grants that focused on underserved groups such as the chronically mentally ill, severely mentally retarded children, the elderly, children, and minorities. The financial incentives to increase services to these neglected groups may draw some resources away from middle-class recipients.

There were other efforts in the late 1970s to limit eligibility for social services to the most needy, particularly in the food stamp program. Started in the early 1960s as a pilot project to assist the indigent, food stamps were originally distributed to fewer than 400,000 persons. The Food Stamp Act of 1964 transformed the pilot project into a national program, which by 1967 was serving almost 1.5 million participants monthly. By 1975 the number of monthly participants had multiplied thirteen-fold to 19.3 million, with the largest increases felt in 1974 and 1975, at which time the program was coming to be known in Congress as the "food stampede." Seeking to rein in this rapid growth, the 1977 amendments to the Food Stamp Act tightened eligibility requirements by disqualifying many students and lowering the income ceilings for participants (for instance, to $10,224 for a family of four).[6] The gross income limit, while stricter than the previous standard, was still about 80% of the national median income in 1975. With an automatic adjustment for inflation the gross income limit reached approximately $14,000 by 1981; at that time the Reagan administration proposed reducing the limit for everyone except elderly and disabled persons to $11,000 for a family of four, which then equaled about 130% of the official poverty level.

Even social insurance, the veritable foundation of the American welfare state, has been hit by proposals to increase selectivity in providing support for the elderly. While conveying the image of an insurance program, the substance of Old Age, Survivors, Disability, and Health Insurance (OASDHI) differs from that of private insurance in several ways. First, the terms of social insurance are established by laws, which Congress can change at any time, unlike contractual relationships between contributors and private insurers. In addition, the compulsory contributions to social insurance resemble more a federal tax than an insurance premium. But the most important distinction is in the relationship between contributions and benefits. Private insurance benefits are computed on the principle of equity, whereby the annuity equals the sum of the contributions plus accumulated interest. In the tight link between contributions and benefits the insured get what they pay for: a fair rate of return. The principle of equity is severely modified by concerns for adequacy in the benefit structure of social insurance. Instead of a fair rate of return, everybody is entitled to more than they paid for in an effort by government to provide an adequate standard of living.

The quest for adequacy in social insurance leads to various inequities as some beneficiaries are entitled to greater federal subsidies than others. The three groups most often cited are recipients of the minimum benefit, the dependents' allowance, and the maximum benefit.

The *minimum benefit*, $122 per month in 1982, gives those who contribute least to the system a proportionately higher return on their contributions than other beneficiaries. While this was designed to

provide a floor of support for low-wage earners and the
employed, a number of minimum benefit recipients are people
primarily covered by alternative pension plans, such as federal civil
service employees, who slip into Social Security to reap the relatively
high returns for minimal payments. There are varying interpretations
concerning the extent to which the minimum benefit is being exploited in this manner.[7]

The *dependents' allowance* increases the covered worker's benefit
by 50% if a spouse is present. Thus, a single worker and a married
worker both contributing the same amount of money over a lifetime
of employment are entitled to substantially different benefits.

The *maximum benefit* is received by high-wage earners with
strong attachments to the labor force. Compared to average and
low-level benefits a smaller proportion of the maximum benefit
represents payment beyond the investment value of contributions.
However, in absolute terms, the subsidy is higher. Thus, high-wage
earners receive a larger amount of unpaid-for benefits than low-wage
earners.[8] In 1982, for example, estimates indicate that the amount of
unpaid-for benefits received by a high-wage earner retiring at age 65
with a dependent spouse would equal $828 per month compared to a
monthly subsidy of only $472 for a low-wage earner in similar
circumstances.[9]

Since the mid-1970s the subsidized portion of Social Security benefits has come under increasing criticism. The issue at heart is: Why
should these benefits be given to many people who are not poor in
order to assure subsidizing those who are poor when there is already
a federal program of Supplemental Security Income (SSI) in place to
provide financial assistance to the elderly poor? Unlike Social Security, the Supplemental Security Income Program employs a means test
to determine recipient eligibility. Policy analysts have seriously debated the merits of redesigning Social Security so that benefits are
directly related to contributions, as in private insurance, and of
transferring the function of providing for adequacy to the more selective SSI program.[10] When it comes to the Social Security system,
however, such radical reform measures tend to generate substantial
opposition. In 1981, for example, Congress decided to eliminate the
minimum benefit only to rescind that action later the same year as
Social Security constituents brought heavy political pressures to bear.

Efforts at more moderate reform were initiated by Congress and passed in 1983. Among the provisions of the 1983 Social Security reform legislation is a tax on benefits which introduces an element of selectivity into the system.[11]

While the period from 1960 to 1980 was generally marked by the spread of middle-class entitlements to social welfare, in the late 1970s the drift toward universalism began to encounter stiff resistance. Citizen tax revolts, spearheaded by Proposition 13 in California, and double digit inflation created economic pressures to contain the expanding welfare state. The 1980 election of a Republican administration bent on reducing government expenditures and stimulating private enterprise was followed by large cuts in social welfare budgets. In the first half of fiscal year 1982, for example, federal appropriations for key human service programs were $2½ billion less than in 1981 and almost $5½ billion below what would have been spent in 1982 if the anticipated increases in program costs had been granted, mainly for food stamps, Medicaid, and programs under the social service block grant.[12] One justification for these cutbacks has been that social provisions should go only to the "truly needy," with the attendant charge that many beneficiaries of the welfare state did not fit into that category.

The sizable reduction of federal spending for social welfare in the early 1980s has fueled a resurgence of selectivity in the allocation of social services. Not only have means-tested eligibility requirements become more stringent, but there is increasing interest in linking consumer charges to the applicant's ability to pay for services. With its concern for determining unit costs, pricing services, and the virtues of "paying one's way," consumer charges appeal to policymakers who support the trend toward commercialization of the social market. The decline of public funding for social welfare lends a strong economic incentive to incorporating new or increased consumer charges in the selective allocation of services.

CHARGING FOR SOCIAL SERVICES

The use of consumer charges is a prevalent feature of the British welfare state. In 1973, fees and charges met almost 15% of the total expenditures for personal social services in England and Wales. The amounts collected by specific services varied considerably; for example, charges for children's homes, homes for the elderly, and other residential care ranged from 16 to 33% of program costs while day centers for adults and meals-on-wheels collected only about 5% of program costs from fees and charges. These figures exaggerate the amount of public savings derived from charges. As Judge points out, the figures include substantial sums that are actually intergovernmental transfers rather than out-of-pocket client contributions.[13] Moreover, the figures do not include the costs of assessing and collecting fees, which must be deducted in any calculation of public savings. Yet after discounting intergovernmental transfers and administrative costs, the British practice of charging for social services is still better developed and yields considerably more income than similar schemes in the United States.

Up until 1975, the major federal efforts to introduce consumer charges in the United States were concentrated on the Headstart and Food Stamp programs. The 1969 amendments to the Economic Opportunity Act called for charging fees in the Headstart program to families with income above the poverty line. The Office of Child Development went so far as actually to develop a fee schedule for Headstart participants. But after hearing that many of the program's participants might not be able to pay for service according to the fee schedule, Congress had second thoughts about this policy. Mandatory charges for Headstart were postponed and later replaced by a policy that simply allowed for voluntary contributions.[14] Consumer charges in the Food Stamp program were reflected in the "purchase requirement," under which participants paid a sum of money to receive food coupons that had a higher cash value; a family of four, for example, might pay up to $146 for $170 worth of food stamps depending upon the family's monthly income. In 1977, however, the purchase requirement for food stamps was eliminated.

The largest existing scheme of consumer charges for social services in the United States was initiated in 1975 under the Title XX program, which was converted into the social services block grant in 1981. Two broad criteria for Title XX service charges stipulate that fees should be reasonably related to the individual's income and not exceed service cost. There is little information available about the percentage of Title XX expenditures met by charges or about the impact of user contribu-

tions on service delivery. What is known, however, is that wide
variations exist among the states in the structuring of fee schedules
and the methods of income assessment.[15] Diverse charging practices
are also found among the local authority social service departments
in Britain.[16]

One of the reasons for the variations in charging practices is that the
problem of designing social service fee schedules lends itself to many
solutions. Charges for private service in the market economy are
generally calculated on the basis of cost plus a margin of profit that
will yield a price competitive with that of other providers. The factors
that must be considered to structure consumer charges in the social
market are more arbitrary than those that inform pricing in the market
economy. The design of fee schedules for services in the social
market involves linking charges to costs and income in the absence of
practical restraints generated by competitive forces and without statutory guidelines regarding how much of the service costs consumers in
different income categories should be required to pay. As a result
social service providers are required to exercise a high degree of
discretion in structuring fee schedules.

While charges for specific services may vary widely in response to
the provider's discretion, the general shape of the price line in fee
schedules takes one of only three basic forms: fixed, notched, or
graduated. These forms are illustrated in Figure 4.1. Each of these
patterns for levying charges affords different benefits in relation to the
degree of efficiency in administering the fee schedule and the degree
of equity in the fee structure.

Fee schedules that incorporate a fixed price line are easy to administer. Under a pattern of fixed charges, once it is determined that
applicants are financially eligible for service, no special administrative efforts are required to tailor fees to individual circumstances.
Moreover, the price line can be set at a level which ensures, at the very
least, that the administrative costs of collecting fees will be met by the
charges levied. One of the untoward features of this approach is that
among applicants who pass the means test, people with the lowest
income are charged the same fee as those with the highest income
who are eligible for the subsidized service. Compared to the other
patterns of charging, fixed fee schedules rank first on administrative
efficiency but are least equitable in relating financial ability to
charges.

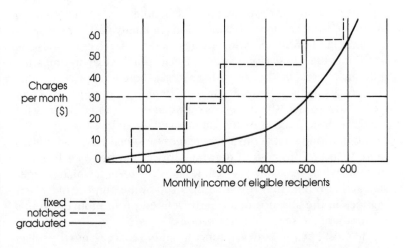

fixed — —
notched – – –
graduated ———

Figure 4.1. Alternative Price Lines for a Service Costing $60 per Month.

Fee schedules based on a graduated price line are costly and time consuming to implement. The price lines in these schedules can form steep arcs or gentle slopes depending upon the assumptions made concerning how the graduated increase in fees should be calibrated with rising family incomes. With fees finely tuned to take into account small changes in family income, this approach is at once the most equitable and administratively inefficient form of charging for services.

The notched price line offers a compromise between fixed and graduated charges which takes some of the edge off their deficiencies as well as their virtues. In having their fees adjusted to income at broad intervals, notched charges are neither as complicated to administer as graduated charges, which vary with small changes in income, nor as simple to administer as fixed charges, which vary not at all. The notched price line results overall in greater equity than fixed charges. However, there is a high degree of inequity built into this fee structure for recipients whose incomes fall just over the cutoff point at each interval. As illustrated in Figure 4.1, for example, recipients with an income of $200 per month would be charged $15 while those earning just a few dollars more would be pushed up to the next level and required to pay $30 for the service.

This brief reconnaissance of consumer charges ignores several other sticky issues in the design of fee schedules, such as determining the unit cost of services, considerations of family size in relation to income, and how to deal with charges for other services in assessing family income. These issues aside, the main point is that in comparing different approaches to computing charges there is no price line that appears distinctly superior for maximizing both administrative efficiency and equity. The trade-offs between equity and efficiency for the three basic price lines are summarized in Table 4.1.

The introduction of consumer charges for social services involves more than the business of drawing a price line between fees and income. Whatever shape a price line takes, the level at which charges start and how high they rise are influenced by the purpose of collecting fees in the absence of a clearly defined profit motive. On this matter there are several interpretations.[17]

The most obvious reason for incorporating charges into the selective allocation of social services is to raise revenue. The wish to gather some additional funds certainly lends impetus to the idea of charges in a period of reduced government support for social welfare. In practice, however, it is difficult to raise substantial revenues through consumer charges. It is often uneconomical to collect very low fees and the benefits of high fees are uncertain. To wit, charges incur administrative costs which low fees may not cover. High fees may defeat their own purpose if they deter immediate demand for service only to have increased demands erupt later as client problems reach an advanced stage that is costlier to treat. High fees may also shift the burdens of public expenditure as low-income applicants are forced to seek additional financial aid from one public agency to help pay the service charges of another. Transfers of this sort take from Peter to pay

Table 4.1. Equity and Efficiency for Alternative Price Lines

Price line	Degree of equity	Degree of administrative efficiency
Fixed	Low	High
Notched	Medium	Medium
Graduated	High	Low

Paul with no real savings to public expenditure. While evidence on the revenue-raising efficacy of consumer charges is limited, Parker's analysis of the British experience indicates that charges for social services usually produce less revenue than anticipated and are of dubious value in reducing public expenditure.[18]

A second purpose of consumer charges is to discourage excessive utilization of services. This purpose derives from the assumption that in the normal course of events there is a tendency among people to abuse free services. Whatever grains of truth there may be in this assumption, it is not entirely clear that consumer charges will induce more careful use of social services. They may have the reverse effect by encouraging trivial demands for service from consumers who feel entitled to get their "money's worth."[19] Moreover, the promiscuous allocation of services does not necessarily follow from the fact that they are offered free of charge. On the contrary, access to most social services requires a diligent interview by professionals who are obligated to assess the nature of the presenting problem and to judge the appropriateness of providing agency resources in light of the applicant's needs. Rather than discouraging unwarranted use of services, charges may simply discourage the consumption of services by those too poor to pay.

The reduction of demand, another objective of consumer charges, is at heart a variation on the theme of restraining abuse. This objective is rarely expressed as a reduction in demand to meet serious and legitimate needs. Instead, the implication of this objective is that the existing level of demand can usually be reduced by fees which would prevent unnecessary and unreasonable use of services.

Finally there are symbolic purposes served by consumer charges which reveal, perhaps, a deeper understanding of their broad appeal than that gleaned from the objectives of raising revenue and checking abuse. By applying principles of the economic market to activities of the welfare state, consumer charges invite the support of those inclined to favor commercialization of the social market. The fact that these principles are highly modified does not detract much from the symbolic significance of pricing services and requiring social welfare recipients to "pay their own way"—even if it is only via intergovernmental transfers routed through their hands.

At the other end of the ideological spectrum, those opposed to capitalist intrusions into the welfare state nevertheless can find some merit in consumer charges as a convenient method to subsidize the poor without stigmatizing them. This social benefit of charges proceeds from the belief that social service recipients are stigmatized by selective eligibility policies, which screen applicants according to their financial means. The symbolic act of paying for service, regardless of how small the contribution, is presumed to lend a certain dignity to recipient status and cast off the stigma supposedly attached to means-tested public aid. For many supporters of the welfare state the assumption that means tests impute stigma is held so firmly that it has almost been compressed into fact. But the facts that have been gathered on this issue suggest a different effect. Several studies have found that the means test per se is not experienced by service recipients as a stigmatizing assault on human dignity.[20] More generally, it may be observed that college students appear virtually unaffected by the means tests often required in making application for financial aid.[21]

What, then, accounts for the persistent assumption that the means test is harmful to recipients' feelings of self-worth? One possibility is that cause and effect are confused. The welfare state traditionally has served many socially unpopular groups such as alcoholics, delinquents, vagrants, paupers, child abusers, and unwed mothers; members of these groups are exposed to varying degrees of societal disapproval before they ever make an application for social welfare benefits. It is improbable that paying a small fee for social services would diminish the stigma frequently attached to these groups. Conversely, it is just as unlikely that consumer charges would do much to improve the basic self-image of groups such as the aged, the disabled, and the blind, toward whom the public is generally sympathetic.[22]

In sum, beyond the practical difficulties of pricing services, the incorporation of consumer charges in the selective allocation of social services must deal with the ambiguities of mixed, sometimes competing, expectations and uncertain outcomes. Consumer charges are no panacea for declining revenues, abuse of services, or the social opprobrium experienced by some social service recipient groups. Although they may offer symbolic affirmation for the values of the market economy, an expansion of consumer charges in the American welfare state would complicate and, perhaps, retard the development of selective policies for allocating services to those deemed most in need and least able to pay for them.

CENTRAL PROBLEM OF SELECTIVITY

In the short run one of the significant difficulties posed by the resurgence of selectivity involves the measurement of need (a difficulty that would be magnified by consumer charges which require estimates not only of financial need but also of the ability to pay specific amounts for service at different levels of income). When universal entitlements gained support between 1960 and 1980, the concept of need was stretched out of the easily identifiable shape that the official federal definition of poverty had lent it in the 1960s. The poor have been replaced by the "truly needy," an ambiguous category that may refer to those with incomes under the official poverty level. Then there are the "near poor," the "working poor" with incomes somewhere between the poverty level and the national median, and the "poor by association," who qualify through residence in low-income areas or membership in low-income groups. There are even those dubbed poor because they feel deprived from observing the standard of living around them and believing they are entitled to the same standard. Both advocates and opponents of selectivity claim special insight into what constitutes the "truly needy," and, as expected, disaffirm each other's wisdom on this matter.

Income has been the traditional yardstick for measuring need. Critics of the welfare state challenge the practice of excluding in-kind benefits in calculating the income of social welfare recipients. They charge that this convention merely exaggerates the degree of poverty in order to increase the size of the welfare state. A Census Bureau study on measuring poverty, released in 1982, lends some weight to this charge. The study examines nine alternative methods for computing the cash value of in-kind social welfare benefits and estimates the effects of this income on figuring the percentage of the population below the poverty line in 1979. Under the most liberal method of evaluating in-kind benefits, which counts the market value of food programs, housing subsidies, and medical aid, only 6.4% of the population would have fallen below the line instead of the official figure of 11.1%, which excludes the value of in-kind benefits.[23] These findings

parallel the previously noted (see chap. 3) results of the 1977 estimates by the Congressional Budget Office, which revealed that the
official poverty figures would be reduced by almost half if the value of
all types of in-kind assistance was taken into consideration.[24]

But the Census Bureau study is attentive to the various assumptions
and complexities involved in measuring the value of in-kind benefits.
Under the study's most restrictive method of assessing in-kind assistance, which excludes the value of all medical benefits, the percentage of those in poverty would have dropped just slightly from 11.1 to
9.8%. One of the problems in making these calculations is that it is
difficult to know how to count medical benefits. If the cash value of
medical assistance is included in calculating a recipient's income, the
sickest poor people with the highest medical bills would appear
almost wealthy in comparison to those in good health.[25]

At the same time that conservative forces press for new ways to
measure family income that include the monetary value of the full
range of social welfare benefits, defenders of the welfare state dispute
the very formula used for drawing the poverty line, which was at
$9,290 for an urban family of four in 1982.[26] They claim that the
poverty line is pegged too low for an adequate level of support and is
improperly indexed to reflect rising standards of living in the United
States. In support of these views are studies that compare the American experience to the way the British poverty line is defined and
indexed, showing American policy in this area to be rather
ungenerous.[27]

In the political and economic climate of the early 1980s the problem of defining the poor and "truly needy" is unlikely to be resolved
in favor of more generous policies for measuring income and need.
Instead, selective criteria for allocating social welfare benefits are
bound to become more stringent as the paring of federal expenditures cuts deeply into the welfare state. The immediate consequences
of increasing selectivity will be to create hardships for many beneficiaries of the welfare state, but in the long run, the resurgence of
selectivity may actually strengthen the welfare state. By directing the
provisions of the social market to those unable to meet their basic
needs through participation in the economic market, selective eligibility criteria in a sense legitimate the welfare state and underscore its
distinctive function in a capitalist society.

In the meantime, as federal resources are withdrawn from the social market it is hoped that the slack will be taken in by increasing mutual aid through family supports and other voluntary alternatives. The pursuit of this hope centers on efforts to strengthen family life and to extend the scope of voluntary social support networks.

NOTES

1. Marc Bendick, Jr., and Mario Cantú, "The Literacy of Welfare Clients," *Social Service Review,* 52 (Mar. 1978), 56–68. Also see Marc Bendick, Jr., "Failure to Enroll in Public Assistance Programs," *Social Work,* 25 (July 1980), 268–80.

2. Richard Titmuss, *Commitment to Welfare* (New York: Pantheon, 1968), p. 196.

3. Kenneth Keniston and Carnegie Council on Children, *All Our Children: The American Family Under Pressure* (New York: Harcourt Brace Jovanovich, 1977), p. 142.

4. Candace Mueller, "Five Years Later A Look at Title XX: The Federal Billion Dollar Social Services Fund," *Grantsmanship Center News* (Nov./Dec. 1980), 36–37.

5. *Federal Register,* 44: 148 (July 31, 1979), 45038.

6. American Public Welfare Association, "The Fiscal Year 1980 Food Stamp Budget," *W-Memo,* Apr. 5, 1979.

7. According to Munnell, "the extent to which dual benefits are received is considerable. It was estimated in 1968 that approximately 40% of those receiving civil service retirement benefits were also receiving Social Security benefits. In direct conflict with its stated welfare objective, the minimum benefit thus often serves to supplement the income of those relatively affluent retirees who receive other pensions" (Alicia Munnell, *The Future of Social Security* [Washington, D.C.: Brookings Institution, 1977], p. 52). In contrast, Berman claims, "rather than this benefit largely going to people who are basically members of another system (the Federal retirement system, for example) or otherwise sufficiently provided for, it turns out that a goodly portion of those receiving the minimum benefit are genuinely low income people" (Jules Berman, "Social Security: Administration Proposals Compared with Congressional Actions," *Washington Social Legislation Bulletin,* 27 [June 8, 1981], 42).

8. Henry Aaron, "Benefits Under the American Social Security System," *Studies in the Economics of Income Maintenance,* ed. Otto Epstein (Washington, D.C.: Brookings Institution, 1976), pp. 49–72; Martha Ozawa, "Income Redistribution and Social Security," *Social Service Review,* 50 (June 1976), 209–23.

9. Martha Ozawa, "Who Receives Subsidies Through Social Security and How Much?" *Social Work,* 27 (Mar. 1982), 131.

10. Munnell, *Future of Social Security,* "What Should be Done to Save Social Security," *Socioeconomic Newsletter,* 7 (Feb./Mar. 1982).

11. Under the 1983 reform bill passed by Congress, 50% of Social Security benefits will be treated as taxable income for retirees whose adjusted gross income plus half their benefits exceeds $25,000 if single and $32,000 if married.

12. David Racine, "Human Services Left $5 Billion Poorer," *Washington Report,* 17 (Feb. 1982), 1–7. The figures cited here do not include the substantial cutbacks in education and housing assistance programs that were made in 1982.

13. Ken Judge, *Rationing Social Services* (London: Heinemann, 1978), pp. 109–31.

14. Joan Miller, *The Development of Fee Schedules*, Human Services Monograph Series, no. 12 (Washington, D.C.: U.S. GPO, 1979), p. 57.

15. Ibid.

16. Ken Judge and James Matthews, *Charging for Social Care: A Case Study of Consumer Charges and the Personal Social Services* (London: Allen & Unwin, 1980).

17. See R. A. Parker, "Charging for Social Services," *Journal of Social Policy*, 5 (Oct. 1976), 359–73, for a perceptive inquiry into the range of purposes attributed to consumer charges.

18. Ibid, p. 362.

19. This point is discussed by Eveline Burns, *Social Security and Public Policy* (McGraw-Hill: New York, 1966), p. 157, and Parker, "Charging for Social Services." Burns also suggests that the responsibility-inducing effect of charges is most likely to exert some positive influence on consumer behavior in programs where the unit of administration is small enough so that excessive utilization of services has a direct and an immediate impact on the rate of charges.

20. See, for example, Martha Ozawa, "Impact of SSI on the Aged and Disabled Poor," *Social Work Research and Abstracts*, 14 (Fall 1978), 3–10; Joel Handler and Ellen Hollingsworth, "How Obnoxious is the 'Obnoxious Means Test'? The View of AFDC Recipients," Institute for Research on Poverty Discussion paper, Madison, University of Wisconsin, Jan. 1969; and Richard Pomeroy and Harold Yahr in collaboration with Lawrence Podell, *Studies in Public Welfare: Effects of Eligibility Investigation on Welfare Clients* (New York: Center for the Study of Urban Problems, City University of New York, 1968).

21. Indeed, at the School of Social Welfare, University of California at Berkeley, students petitioned for the means test to be the *main criterion* for determining the award of fellowships.

22. For a more detailed analysis of the assumption that stigma results from means-tested social welfare programs, see Neil Gilbert and Harry Specht, *Dimensions of Social Welfare Policy* (Englewood Cliffs: Prentice-Hall, 1974), pp. 64–65.

23. Timothy Smeeding, *Alternative Methods for Valuing Selected In-Kind Transfer Benefits and Measuring Their Effects on Poverty*, U.S. Bureau of the Census, Technical Paper no. 50 (Washington, D.C.: U.S. GPO, 1982).

24. U.S. Congress, Congressional Budget Office, *Poverty Status of Families Under Alternative Definitions of Income* (Washington, D.C.: U.S. GPO, June 1977).

25. Smeeding, *Alternative Methods.*

26. For some of the flavor of this controversy see "Measuring Poverty: A Debate," *Public Welfare*, 36 (Spring 1978), 46–55.

27. Sidney E. Zimbalist, "Recent British and American Poverty Trends: Conceptual and Policy Contrasts," *Social Service Review*, 51 (Sept. 1977), 419–33; Donald E. Chambers, "Another Look at Poverty Lines in England and the United States," *Social Service Review*, 55 (Sept. 1981), 472–82.

PART III

VOLUNTARY ALTERNATIVES

FIVE

DILEMMAS OF FAMILY POLICY

With the advent of the market economy and the welfare state, private enterprise and public agencies assumed many of the social functions performed in earlier times by the family. As these institutions joined in mediating between the individual and society, an uncomfortable union has evolved in the family's relationship to the welfare state and the market economy. It is, as we shall see, a tangled relationship which spawns policies that purport to enhance family life at the same time that they threaten to weaken the traditional bonds of family unity.

The welfare state's disposition toward family life is a confused mix of humanitarian sentiments and the egalitarian aspirations of collectivism. Preservation of the family, as an institution that nurtures the young and satisfies many basic human needs, has an intrinsic appeal to the humanitarian sentiments of collectivists. However, the family is also the main institutional vehicle through which privilege is transmitted from one generation to the next. Strengthening this link of privilege runs counter to the egalitarian temperament of collectivism. When obligations and affections of kinship take precedence over loyalty to the community, the investment of family energies and resources is often at odds with collectivist objectives.

While collectivists are ambivalent about the family, as an institution it appears to hold a favored position in capitalist society. One strong motive for future-oriented entrepreneurial activity is drawn from the bonds of family life. As Schumpeter observed, these bonds form a mainspring of the capitalist spirit;[1] they sustain the bourgeois drive to plan, invest, and sacrifice for a future in which children will benefit from the gratifications their parents postponed.

In a sense, the family motive complements the Protestant ethic as an explanation of capitalist behavior. According to the Protestant ethic, capitalist activity is almost a religious calling. The accumulation of wealth is evidence of virtue, promising salvation in the hereafter. Ultimately, however, salvation in the hereafter remains an uncertain proposition. If it fails to materialize, not all is lost as long as the family motive also impels the capitalist spirit. For, whatever transpires in the hereafter, the bourgeois legacy of wealth most certainly provides a roof of economic security to shelter the family line here on earth.

While the bonds of family life may support the spirit of capitalism, it has been observed that extensive family bonds can undermine capitalism in practice. The many ties of an extended family network have a devitalizing effect upon entrepreneurial activity, as obligations to assist kin tend to increase with profits.[2] The budding entrepreneur must then choose between familial duty and the wish to invest in the growth of the firm. There is some evidence that the impact of the extended family on entrepreneurial activity is mixed. On the one hand, relatives can facilitate the entrepreneur's start in life through pooling of resources to help launch the business. On the other hand, the extended family network may hinder expansion of this firm by numerous claims on a share of the profits once the business is established.[3] Thus, in general, it is the small, mobile, tightly knit nuclear family unit rather than the extended kinship network that is often perceived as the essential human cell of capitalist society.

At one time the nuclear family was believed to be the product of modern industrial society, which first arose in Western Europe. According to this belief, the transition from rural feudalism to urban industrial life led to the collapse of a preindustrial family pattern characterized by early marriage, communal living arrangements that encompassed a wide circle of kin, and close ties between these coresident family groups. In place of that family system, the modern nuclear family emerged, built upon relatively late marriages (in the middle or late twenties) that formed small conjugal units living under a separate roof, with kinship ties concentrated on a narrow base of filial responsibility. Studies of the history of the family, however, reveal that these central features of the "modern" nuclear family were widespread in Western Europe centuries before the Industrial Revolution.[4] Because these elements have endured for that length of time it is perhaps more appropriate to speak of the traditional nuclear family, a unit whose stability and vitality in modern times have been battered by high rates of divorce, illegitimacy, and infertility.

With attenuation of the family unit, the entrepreneurial drive is deprived of a powerful motivating force. Schumpeter was among the

first economists to claim a connection between the erosion of traditional family values and parenthood, and the progressive decline of
capitalism. Writing in the late 1930s his comments on the deterioration of family life were based, in part, on the rising number of
childless marriages witnessed after World War I—a trend which led
many social analysts of that period to envision a declining future for
the nuclear family. This prognosis improved measurably after World
War II with the rising marriage rates, baby boom, and general resurgence of familism. Since the mid-1960s, however, family life in America
has dissolved in a turn of events that lends almost prescient vision to
many of Schumpeter's observations.

Although less deterministic in tone and considerably less sanguine
about the eventual breakdown of capitalism, Schumpeter's analysis
agreed with that of Marx in predicting that the capitalist system was
headed for destruction. Unlike Marx, however, he saw this outcome
as due not to the failure of capitalism as an economic system but
rather to its success, which eventually would undermine the attitudes,
values, and entrepreneurial behavior that gave the system its vitality
and moral force.

Variations on this theme—that the commercial success of capitalism contains the seeds of its own undoing—have echoed across the
decades. Bell observes how the Protestant ethic was undermined by
the capitalist invention of instant credit: "Previously one had to save
in order to buy. But with credit cards one could indulge in instant
gratification. The system was transformed by mass production and
mass consumption, by the creation of new wants and new means of
gratifying those wants. . . . When the Protestant ethic was sundered
from bourgeois society, only hedonism remained, and the capitalist
system lost its transcendental ethic."[5] In a similar vein Heilbroner
claims that the moral cement of capitalism "is dissolving in its commercial ethic."[6]

According to Schumpeter, the material success and widespread
adoption of the capitalist viewpoint invite the deterioration of family
values. That success promotes the rationalization of human behavior
through which individuals are inexorably led to weigh the costs and
benefits of prospective actions. In the emerging system of human cost
accounting the concrete sacrifices of parenthood and family life are
thrown into bold relief. After all, the creation of a family is more an

emotional response to deep-seated yearnings and a moral tradition than a rational choice to maximize a life of wealth and comfort. Children are no longer the economic assets they were on the family farm; instead, raising a family is an expensive proposition; the Department of Agriculture estimates the costs of rearing children from birth to age 18 at $76,655 for an urban family of moderate income in the western United States.[7] Beyond the economic costs, parenthood carries a heavy burden of social responsibility; it is a dirty, noisy business that engenders loss of personal freedom and interferes with the woman's pursuit of a worldly career. On the other side of the ledger, alternative life-styles promise increased free time and the money to enjoy it, the comforts and services of condominium living, exotic vacations, fast and light traveling (unencumbered by pampers, folding cribs, and other paraphernalia of family excursions), and multiple adult relationships based on the pleasure of their company.

But the balance sheet is incomplete. For, as Schumpeter observed incisively almost 50 years ago, "the greatest of the assets, the contribution made by parenthood to physical and moral health—to 'normality' as we might express it—particularly in the case of women, almost invariably escapes the rational searchlight of modern individuals who, in private as in public life, tend to focus attention on ascertainable details of immediate utilitarian relevance and to sneer at the idea of hidden necessities of human nature or the social organism."[8] Since these benefits of physical and moral health—fulfillment of the "hidden necessities of human nature"—elude the cost accounting of parenthood, individual calculations based on rational interest generate little support for establishing a family home. On the bottom line, the joys of parenthood dim in contrast to the gusty attractions of alternative life-styles.

As the family motive declines, the entrepreneur's attitudes and values are no longer shaped by transcendental ambitions. Instead, Schumpeter argued, these ambitions acquire circumspect and temporal qualities that afford more of an incentive to take the pleasures of the moment, made so readily available by the productive success of capitalism, than to work long hours, save, invest, and accumulate wealth for the benefit of future generations. In this process the drive to accumulate wealth is displaced by the urge for increased consumption, as hedonistic impulses press hard against the waning constraints of family responsibility. Gilder's observation that contemporary research reveals "husbands work 50% harder than bachelors of comparable age, education and skills" adds a resonant voice to the distant strains of Schumpeter's discourse on the centrality of the nuclear family to capitalist productivity.[9]

Yet there is another interpretation of these developments. The erosion of family life may be more compatible with the evolution of capitalism than is suggested by Schumpeter's analysis. Childless couples indeed engage in life-styles marked by high levels of material consumption. Similarly, single-parent families and detached individuals multiply the demands for shelter, household goods, and an array of out-of-home services including laundry, meals, daycare, and entertainment. They are smaller, more mobile, units than the intact nuclear family. Having only themselves to rely on for economic support, these adults are under pressure to join the labor market; they not only add to the flexibility of an industrial labor force, they substantially increase the size of the pool. Thus, the decline of traditional family life is accompanied by increases in both market demands for goods and services and the labor force necessary to produce for these markets. These are not conditions under which capitalism will necessarily wither away.

Schumpeter was, of course, correct in observing that the engine of capitalist production is fueled by entrepreneurial leadership, disciplined patterns of saving, and investment to create the means for increased productivity and greater surplus in the future. But to run smoothly this engine also requires a large, adaptable labor force and markets for its output. If most people postponed gratification and saved to invest in their own business, wage labor and markets for the products of these capitalist enterprises would be sorely depleted.

To conclude that the erosion of family life necessarily undermines capitalism ignores three salient considerations. First, as noted, the breakdown of family enlarges both the supply of wage labor and the demand for capitalist goods. Second, even in the 1980s with the divorce rate approaching one in two marriages and the average family size down to 3.28, the family motive remains firmly rooted in a large portion of the adult population. The erosion of family may be widespread but it is hardly universal. Moreover, as Carlson points out, the model of the bourgeois nuclear family was an ideal form that never

extended to a majority of American households.[10] To the extent that
the family motive inspires disciplined patterns of entrepreneurial
behavior, its force, though diminished, is still sufficiently extensive to
sustain a broad base of entrepreneurial activity in capitalist society.
Finally, inherent in the dissolution of family life are certain opportunities for increasing labor force loyalty to and dependence upon the
work place. As we shall see, in the 1980s family-oriented business
policies are among the popular efforts proposed to buttress traditional patterns and responsibilities of family life.

HUMANITARIAN AND EGALITARIAN DILEMMAS OF FAMILY POLICY

The welfare state's response to the erosion of family life in the United
States is beclouded by collectivists' ambivalence toward this institution. Opinions differ about the most desirable conditions of family
life and how to achieve it; these differences run deep, muddling both
the means and ends of family policy. Although there are many complex issues, much of the disagreement surrounding family policy can
be traced to two basic dilemmas that have come to the fore since
family life entered the spotlight of public debate in the late 1970s.

The first dilemma inherent in the design of family policy is that of
the "helping hand." Social insurance, for example, in extending
financial benefits and health care to the elderly reduces the pressures
on children to discharge their traditional obligation of parental care
and support in old age. Eventually the state replaces the family as the
major provider for the elderly. While social security financing represents an intergenerational transfer through which benefits paid to the
retired elderly are contributed by their children's generation, it is a
transfer mediated by the state. The intentions are humane. The problem is that in the process of extending the range of social and
economic assistance to those in need, humanitarian activities of the
welfare state frequently reduce the family's traditional responsibility
to provide for its members.[11] In this regard it is interesting to point out
that in the literature on the family, state, and market economy, the
expansion of the welfare state is indicted for eroding the traditional
values and norms of family life perhaps as often as is the success of
capitalism.

The humanitarian dilemma is complicated by the fact that the
results of public interventions aimed at helping families are often

difficult to predict, and when known are open to varied interpretations. Day-care programs provide the type of social supports that ease the strains of child rearing and allow both parents to pursue independent careers. Advocates for the universal provision of day-care perceive the program affording social, psychological, and economic benefits to family life along the following lines: with two incomes the family's economic security increases; parents may spend less time with their children, but the time spent is of higher quality as many of the drab daily chores of child rearing are handled at the day-care center; psychologically, both parents feel good about themselves as worthy and independent adults capable of earning a living and maintaining relationships with other adults in the business world; and the children benefit from the collective experience of being around other youngsters at an early age. According to this view, child-care provisions that support the movement of wives into the labor force contribute to the happiness and well-being of the family unit.

An alternative and more critical view challenges the presumed social and economic benefits of a two-paycheck family. Scrutiny of the economic benefits reveals that work-related expenses and increased taxes due to the higher bracket into which the second salary pushes family income consume 34% of a wife's earnings in a two-paycheck family.[12] Despite these heavy costs, a working wife obviously increases the family's income.[13] Whether this increases the family's financial security is another matter.

A family's sense of financial security hinges upon both the regular income available to meet current costs of living and the stock of resources that can be drawn upon for survival in case of future hardships. As the wife's labor becomes a steady source of income, the two-earner family often comes to depend just as heavily on that additional money for on-going support as on the husband's earnings. While securing a higher income to meet current costs of living, the two-earner family forfeits the long-run flexibility of a full-time homemaker family, which holds the wife's earning capacity in reserve as a kind of insurance against future economic emergencies. Thus, the question arises: Is the degree of financial security that accompanies the higher earnings of a two-paycheck family more comforting than the degree of security that comes with having a wife's market potential kept in reserve?[14]

In calculating the economic costs and benefits of a two-earner family it is also necessary to take into account the loss of services traditionally performed by the full-time homemaker; estimates on the average cash value of these services in 1980 range from $9,410 to $12,000 a year.[15] Over the family life cycle the homemaker's value is highest during the child-rearing period and declines in later years. Working parents, of course, continue to perform many domestic services such as shopping, cleaning, and preparation of family meals. These activities, however, lengthen the overall amount of work time taken on by employed wives who are usually cast in the homemaker role after a day at the office. A study of household labor indicates that employed wives perform 61% of all housework in comparison to the 72% of all housework performed by full-time homemakers. The principal difference in domestic activities found between these groups is that employed wives spent considerably less time caring for family members, particularly children.[16]

Critics of day-care services that facilitate the trend toward two-career families are skeptical about the economic benefits that result after the costs of day care, work-related expenses, taxes, and the loss of leisure time are subtracted from the wife's earnings. As for the social consequences, they take a dim view of the notion that the less time working parents spend with their children somehow invests the experience with a "higher quality." There is also concern that as the use of day-care centers increases, a large measure of the traditional responsibility for socialization in the decisive years of early childhood will shift from the family to agencies of the state or private sector. Finally, and most important, day-care adversaries fear that by reducing the degree of social and economic interdependence among family members, day-care provisions would also scrape away at some of the basic adhesion of family life.

Similar problems of sorting out the contrary effects of social welfare policies on family life are associated with proposals for guaranteed minimum incomes, regularly put forth as programs to cushion the severe economic pressures on low-income families. Financial stress is recognized as among the major factors that increase the risk of marital dissolution.[17] By assuring families a reliable source of financial aid without the stigma of public assistance, the guaranteed minimum income program holds out the promise to strengthen and stabilize family life. A competing hypothesis, however, suggests that in providing wives with an alternative means of support that would supply the same level of resources outside marriage as within, the guaranteed minimum income reduces the material incentives to stay married.[18]

These hypotheses were tested empirically in the Seattle and Denver Income Maintenance Experiments (SIME/DIME). As mentioned earlier (see chap. 2), this significant study drew on a sample of 4,706 cases; there were 11 experimental groups, each of which received one of three guaranteed levels of support—$3,800, $4,800, or $5,600; and these grants were taxed at varying rates. The study's results offer strong support for the proposition that a guaranteed income program decreases marital stability. Compared to that for the control group, the probability of divorce for the experimental group at the $3,800 level of support was 63% higher for blacks, 184% higher for whites, and 83% higher for Chicanos. Overall the rate of marital dissolution for experimental families was approximately twice that of control group families.[19]

There were, however, some anomalies in the findings, especially the puzzling fact that the marital dissolution rates for each ethnic group at the high support level ($5,600) were less than those at the lower levels of support.[20] According to theory the opposite should occur. If the degree of financial independence available to wives outside marriage contributes to the risk of divorce, then at higher levels of financial support these risks should increase. Also it is difficult to explain the huge differences in dissolution rates between experimental families at the lowest level of support ($3,800) and control group families, since in financial terms a comparable level of support outside marriage was available to the control group wives under existing income maintenance programs, mainly AFDC and food stamps.[21] Finally, while the study reveals the short-term consequences of guaranteed incomes, the program's long-term effects on marital stability remain unknown. After the first round of divorces by all those inclined to dissolve their marriage in response to the opportunity for outside support, it is conceivable that the new divorce rates for the remaining pool of married couples would be lower than current rates.[22]

Even if there were unequivocal evidence that family-oriented programs such as day care and the guaranteed minimum income had a destabilizing influence on married life, by eroding social obligations and economic interdependence, there are those for whom such findings would be interpreted in support of these programs. Many proponents of family policy see little inherent virtue in marital stability, sharing, as Rossi puts it, "the common view that the nuclear family and monogamous marriage are oppressive, sexist, 'bourgeois,' and sick."[23] They believe that no strand in the bonds of family life should be knit from traditional social obligations and economic interdependence; rather family bonds are seen as human relationships that individuals choose to sustain essentially because it pleases them to do so. Thus, when a relationship no longer works, the bond dissolves and the partners are free to leave in search of more compatible arrangements including "variant families" of which there are many types, all deserving equal recognition and social support.[24] This perspective represents an egalitarian view of human relationships that gives rise to the second major dilemma of family policy.

The egalitarian dilemma is illustrated in President Carter's formal announcement of the White House Conference on Families (WHCF), which cited two of the "growing problems" confronted by American families: "Two out of five marriages now end in divorce. One child in eight is born outside of marriage." While indicating that these problems need to be addressed, the statement goes on to promise that the conference will also recognize the pluralism of family life in America: "There are families in which several generations live together, families with *two parents or one* and families with or without children. The Conference will respect this diversity"[25] (emphasis added). Clearly, one-parent families are with few exceptions the result of divorce, desertion, and children born out of wedlock—the "growing problems" that Carter's statement previously identified. Is the one-parent family a problem to be rectified or an expression of diversity to be respected, perhaps even encouraged?

The discrepancy in these statements reflects a dilemma of family policy engendered by the egalitarian zeal of welfare state advocates, which dictates even treatment to all forms of human relationships. From the egalitarian perspective traditional stable family arrangements are no more preferable than newer, more fluid, and unconventional forms. According to this view, all forms from homosexual unions to communal families satisfy some human needs, have strengths and weaknesses, and deserve public sanction and whatever benefits family policies might offer.

This desire for family policies that treat everyone equally leads to some curious definitions of *family* as a category for the allocation of social benefits. The Department of Housing and Urban Development, for example, has a category of *Single Person Family* (the final evolution of the nuclear family), which is eligible for low-income housing; similarly, family memberships in New York's Metropolitan Museum are available to any two people living at the same address or two people who live apart (the "nuclear fission" family) but agree to have membership forms sent to one address. And social workers are advised to adopt a "unifying framework" in clinical intervention with divorced families through which "the divorce process can be viewed as a series of transitions that mark the family's change from married to divorced, from nuclearity to binuclearity. Rather than dissolving the family, divorce creates the need to develop a new equilibrium over time, with specific structural and behavioral rules."[26]

The egalitarian dilemma, on the one hand, is that if the definition of *family* becomes a vessel into which any human arrangement can be poured, there is little basis to distinguish family policy from any other policy that might promote social welfare. On the other hand, the identification of preferable family arrangements that public policies would aim to strengthen perforce results in some groups receiving greater public support and encouragement than others. There is also the accompanying danger that families not fitting the preferred mold would be stigmatized and discriminated against.

This, of course, is only a dilemma for those primarily concerned with designing policies that directly address family well-being. As suggested earlier, there is some ambivalence toward conventional family life among collectivist supporters of the welfare state. Garbed in the politically redoubtable cloak of "family policy," the egalitarian perspective often masks a deeper collectivist commitment to extend the reach of the welfare state, to attack poverty, and to increase the redistribution of wealth in society.

Although well represented, the egalitarian perspective holds no monopoly over debates on family policy. Support for traditional viewpoints that favor the stable nuclear family is still considerable.[27]

Indeed, shortly after President Carter's announcement, the White House Conference on Families was postponed when advocates of the traditional perspective challenged the symbolic propriety of the appointment of a divorcée with three children as the conference's executive director. Consequently, the conference was rescheduled with a new executive director (whose intact family status was less compromising) and a new format under which the conference was decentralized. The new format emphasized taking the conference to the people through a series of state and regional meetings rather than holding one major national forum in Washington, D.C., as originally planned.

Disbursing the conference among state and regional gatherings reduced the potential for national mobilization around controversial issues which might have developed in the original scheme to hold one big event. As would be expected, the revised format produced an impressive amount of activity. At the state level more than 500 hearings, conferences, and other forums were conducted, generating about 5,000 recommendations. Nowhere are the dilemmas and conflicts surrounding family policy in the United States revealed more vividly than in the net results of the 1980 White House Conference on Families.

THE WHITE HOUSE CONFERENCE: SOMETHING FOR EVERYONE

The round of activities at the state level were only preliminary events in the WHCF. The main events, which followed, included three regional White House Conferences in Baltimore, Minneapolis, and Los Angeles, representing the eastern, middle, and western states. Altogether, about 2,000 delegates attended these conferences and adopted more than 150 recommendations. After these regional events a 117-member National Task Force met in Washington, D.C., to summarize the conference recommendations, the top 20 of which were as follows:

1. A call for family-oriented personnel policies—flextime, leave policies, shared and part-time jobs, transfer policies. (92.7%)
2. New efforts to prevent alcohol and drug abuse—education and media initiatives. (92.7%)
3. Major changes in the tax code to eliminate the marriage tax penalty, revise inheritance taxes, and recognize homemakers. (92.1%)

4. Tax policies to encourage home care of aging and handicapped persons. (92.0%)
5. Greater assistance to families with a handicapped member—tax credits, financial help, etc. (91%)
6. A call for systematic analysis of all laws, regulations and rules for their impact on families. (90.4%)
7. Efforts to increase public awareness and sensitivity towards persons with handicapping conditions. (90.1%)
8. Government efforts to assist handicapped persons—enforce existing laws, etc. (89.8%)
9. Encourage independence and home care for aging persons—tax incentives, housing programs. (89%)
10. More equitable economic treatment of full-time homemakers—Social Security changes, programs for displaced homemakers. (87.4%)
11. Reform of Social Security—eliminate biases against families, marriage, homemakers. (84.9%)
12. Increased pressure on media to curb excess violence, sex, stereotypes. (83.4%)
13. Increased efforts to combat employment discrimination (83%)
14. Support for family violence prevention efforts and services. (82%)
15. Involvement of families in improved family support services and self-help efforts. (81.5%)
16. Support for full employment—implement Humphrey–Hawkins Act, job creation efforts. (81.4%)
17. Development of coherent energy and inflation policy. (79.4%)
18. Promote and support a variety of child care choices—home, community and center based, parental choice. (79%)
19. Improved tax incentives for family housing. (78.3%)
20. Increased efforts to prevent and deal with adolescent pregnancy. (77.9%)[28]

This list touches upon virtually every item in the welfare state agenda since the New Deal. It is a typical smorgasbord that serves something for everyone, mostly composed of common recipes, prepared beforehand, and without claim to excellence. The fare is not surprising. What is surprising, however, is that while these recommendations for family policy offer something for everyone, there is relatively little here to nourish and support the traditional nuclear family as a child-rearing unit. About half the recommendations address alcohol and drug abuse, the handicapped, unemployment, racial and sexual discrimination, energy and inflation policy, media excesses, housing, and various approaches to income maintenance. Amid the swarm of recommendations, voices calling for specific provisions for the formation and sustenance of family life—such as the marriage loans and assistance programs found in Czechoslovakia and Austria, the family vacations provided in France, and the comprehensive maternity benefits that are a staple of family support in many European countries—are conspicuous by their absence.[29] Recommendations that seem to address the family unit directly lean more toward providing incentives and support for working mothers and single parents than toward sustaining intact families in which mothers might prefer to stay home and perform traditional child-care and homemaking functions. Expressions of interest for the special problems of two-parent families with a large number of children are rare. In fact, regard for children in general is mentioned in the summary report about as often as are concerns for supporting racial and ethnic diversity. A rough word count indicates 73 references to children and 66 to racial and ethnic minorities.

As broad as it may appear, the summarized list of recommendations does not accurately reflect the extensive social welfare agenda represented by this list. Regarding the recommendation for meeting family housing needs, for example, the report elaborates on the truly inclusive scope of the adopted proposals:

Among other approaches to meeting housing needs, the delegates called for tax incentives, subsidies, and reduced interest rates. They called for strict enforcement of current laws and passage of new legislation to outlaw discrimination against families with children, against minorities, single persons, and because of age and other characteristics including handicapping conditions, sexual preference, and blood and legal relationships. This discrimination also should be prohibited by all local and federal housing and financing programs, except those projects exclusively directed to provide housing for elderly persons. The Minneapolis proposal urged priority action on migrant, Indian, rural and low income housing in ghettos and barrios.

Minneapolis and Los Angeles called for an end to restrictive zoning practices. Minneapolis urged an overhaul of federal housing programs to produce more units and called for an end to practices which restrict the supply of housing and fair access to housing, such as red lining. Baltimore delegates (90%) emphasized the preservation of a sense of neighborhood through efforts to increase home ownership, develop effective housing code enforcement and avoid displacement of families. Each Conference urged more effective programs of housing maintenance or code enforcement.[30]

The recommendations on inflation and energy policies are equally sweeping. The report reveals that:

> More than three-fourths of the delegates voted that special emphasis on inflation be given to the cost of food, health care, energy, and housing. Delegates opposed anti-inflation efforts at the expense of human services and opposed attempting to slow inflation by increasing unemployment. They also called for a coherent energy policy, support of mass transit, a comprehensive national health care program, and lower interest rates to enable families to buy homes and meet other family needs.[31]

At the same time that the message to halt inflation was forcefully delivered, the delegates also called loudly for reduced taxes and increased benefits in various programs. The recommendations voiced by the WHCF cover almost everything but a cure for cancer, and even that is not completely excluded as 79% of the delegates at the Los Angeles conference recommended that the government discontinue subsidy of the tobacco industry. In sum, the 100-page summary of the WHCF, complete with photographs, sketches, and graphs, is so densely shaded by expansive goals of the welfare state that future historians studying twentieth-century family life in the United States will be hard pressed to reconstruct how or why contemporary American families function based on the contents of *Listening to American Families.*

Coherence, relevance, and practicality may be inappropriate standards against which to judge the final recommendations of the White House Conference on Families. Those sophisticated in the ways of White House Conferences of this sort know that they are often symbolic political events meant to convey a message of national concern. If in this case the message got garbled, as concerns for family life were joined to a stunning array of peripheral issues, it might be said that the conference served its purpose nevertheless.

However, beneath the litany of sweeping concern for family life, the WHCF delivers another message which continuously bubbles to the surface. Plainly put, the message is that the welfare state must meet the pressing needs of individuals and groups, but there is no particular style or form of family life that merits its support. This message may be interpreted as a "neutral" position on family policy. It may also be seen as an effort to advance pluralistic forms of family life. But for those to whom the meaning of family life centers on the values of marriage and child rearing, the message appears to promote nothing less than the anarchy toward which family life seems headed.

TURNING TO BUSINESS

The last decade has seen rapid growth in the delivery of social services in work settings under the auspices of business. As noted earlier, there were approximately 2,000 employee assistance programs established between 1972 and 1978.[32] And estimates indicate that by 1980 the total number of such programs was more than 5,000 nationwide.[33] These programs offer a broad range of social services dealing with many of the problems—alcohol, drug, marital, legal, psychological, medical, financial, and housing—that traditionally (at least since the 1930s) have fallen within the purview of the American welfare state.

The expansion of privately sponsored social welfare activity is part of the general trend toward commercialization of the social market, which marks the course of welfare capitalism emerging in the 1980s. In line with this trend, among the numerous recommendations put forth at the White House Conference on Families, the one to receive highest priority addressed policies for the work place. Business is called upon to develop family-oriented work policies such as flex time, job sharing, maternal leave, and child-care arrangements. These policies, it is suggested, will not only benefit the family but will also help to reduce absenteeism and to increase productivity.

The main thrust of family-oriented business policies is directed toward the needs of two-career households and single working parents. In both cases these policies facilitate the shift of a parent's, usually the mother's, labor from the home to the market economy. While flex time, maternal leave, and child-care arrangements make it easier for parents to work and raise children at the same time, the impact of these policies on the stability of family life is uncertain. With the economic benefits and social stimulation of independent careers, a married couple may find greater happiness in their relationship. However, by providing each spouse a source of financial support and social assistance in areas such as legal services, housing, and particularly, child-care services outside marriage, work-place benefits reduce the traditional degree of interdependence in family life. The increased risk of divorce arising from this "independence effect" cannot be readily discounted, as evidenced by the results of the guaranteed income experiments.

But the immediate independence both parents acquire through employment and family-oriented work-place policies is in a larger sense paradoxical. What autonomy spouses may gain in their relationships to each other and the family unit, they lose through increased social and economic dependence on the market economy for meeting many of their individual and family needs, which were previously satisfied within the privacy of the home. Increasing the range of family activities that are conducted through what are essentially market transactions depletes the family bonds forged by daily interactions and joint responsibilities of home life. There are, of course, many positive consequences to the reform of business settings that make them more flexible and responsive to individual schedules and family needs. The point is that those policies may do more to enhance individual convenience than to strengthen family life.

In calling upon business to design family-oriented policies it is important to recognize that there is very little about traditional family life that is inherently advantageous to the market economy. Isolated individuals are more dependent on the market to satisfy their consumption needs, a point that is driven home by a Berkeley sociologist, a bachelor who dedicated his book to the staffs of a house cleaning service, three restaurants, a local laundry, and an auto repair service. The market economy expands when a wife's labor is redirected from the family dinner table to the fast food chain. And if married men tend to work harder than bachelors, divorce increases the overall size of the labor pool, and single working parents with children in the firm's child-care program are likely to be motivated employees.

There is in this turn to business a sense of déja vu. On the surface family-oriented work-place policies proposed for the 1980s differ somewhat from the industrial welfare programs that spread throughout the United States at the turn of the twentieth century. Beneath the programmatic forms, however, these past and present activities share the looming embrace of industrial paternalism. For the single working parent and the two-career household, today's family-oriented business policies advance a subtle form of paternalism that in its own way may be as influential on the texture of family life as was the company town invented in the earlier days of capitalism.

AN ALTERNATIVE PERSPECTIVE: IN SUPPORT OF DOMESTICITY

It is tempting to conclude from the various proposals for family policy in the 1980s that both the welfare state and the market economy stand actively opposed to the traditional values and norms of family life. This conclusion implies hidden motives in the design of family policy proposals that are consciously aimed at undermining the traditional nuclear family. To some people such a conspiracy no doubt offers a plausible explanation for the perverse contradictions of policies that diminish conjugal bonds in the name of strengthening family life. However, the conspiracy theory of family policy imposes a clarity of purpose and resolve on a policy area muddled by mixed motives and ambivalent sentiments.

A more accurate conclusion is that the nuclear family is the victim of passive neglect rather than active opposition. There is little about the patterns of traditional family life that elicit enthusiastic support from either the welfare state or the market economy. In contrast, as already suggested, isolated individuals, single parent families, and other variant family forms are likely to create more demand for the goods and services of both the welfare state and the market economy. Family policies from those quarters are thus inclined to flow with the tide of women's liberation and the currents of egalitarian thought on alternative family forms.

Until recently the nuclear family held a revered position in American culture. It stood, as Carlson observes, "as the ideal form of American family life, as the measure of normality or deviance, and as the mark of responsibility and respectability."[34] It was supported in this position by most other American social institutions. However, since the mid-1960s distinctions between normality and deviance have fallen into disrepute, giving way to egalitarian appraisals of "alternative" life-styles; the dowdy virtues of responsibility and respectability have lost their following; and the nuclear family not only has been abandoned as the ideal form of family life, but even its desirability is questioned by the more extreme advocates of the alternative life-styles.

In place of the ideal-type nuclear family, a range of alternative family forms has gained social legitimacy and public support under the liberal umbrella of family policy. Motherhood, child rearing, all the other work associated with domesticity, and the interdependence of husband and wife that comes with the conventional division of labor in family life are accorded faint recognition and low esteem in the schemes of alternative family life-styles. These alternative schemes place high value on a career for women. They are endorsed by the types of policies that favor performance of child-rearing and other domestic functions outside the home, thereby assisting wives and mothers to enter the labor force. It would stretch the point to say that these so called family-oriented policies have caused the restructuring of family life. Clearly, there are larger social and economic forces at work molding alternative family forms. It is within the larger cultural context that family-oriented policies offer both an explicit response to the needs generated by these new family arrangements and an implicit inducement to their continued formation.

Few proposals made in the name of family-oriented policies reinforce traditional family bonds or enhance the quality of domestic life. Nevertheless, these policies represent valid and important efforts to help families adjust to contemporary social and economic demands, especially those upon women. Many women enter the labor market under the press of necessity. A nationwide Gallup survey reveals that women indicate financial need as the main reason for working twice as often as personal satisfaction. When the survey asked about alternatives they would envision as providing the most interesting and satisfying life, 55% of the women who wanted to be married and have children did not wish a full-time job or career outside the home.[35] These findings are somewhat at odds with the general impression one receives from the media and women's liberation spokespeople that working women are on the high road to freedom and self-realization. For most men and women the personal rewards of work are considerably less than those secured by authors, professors, lawyers, movie stars, politicians, and other personalities in the media and the forefront of the women's liberation movement—who tout what appears from their vantage points, the obvious attractions of labor in the marketplace over housework activities.

There are compelling reasons, of course, for women to work out-side the household. Paid employment confers status which, however meager, is higher than that of housework and child rearing. The demise of neighborhood schools, high rates of mobility, fewer moth-ers staying at home, and corporate takeover of local enterprises contribute to the increasingly impersonal character of community life; full-time homemakers in the 1980s thus experience a higher degree of social isolation than in previous generations; joining the labor force often offers an escape from the engulfing anonymity of household work. Above all, a wife's employment improves the fami-ly's economic position in society; in 1977 the median income for families with working wives was $20,722 compared to $15,796 for families in which the husband was the only wage earner.[36]

The search for status, material well-being, social integration, and a higher calling has led many housewives to shift their labor from the home to the marketplace. Although there are benefits to this trend, they accrue not without costs to the quality of family life. These costs include the reduction of time and energy devoted to leisure activities, child–parent interactions, and the personalized care and attention to family members that only a full-time homemaker can provide. The principal approach of proposals for family-oriented policies in the United States is to compensate for the various costs to family life which are associated with the absence of a full-time homemaker. This approach to family policy has meaningful consequences for parents and children adjusting to new family arrangements that involve the contraction of domestic life.

There is another perspective on family policy that has been largely ignored by social welfare planners. This approach compensates not for the absence but for the presence of a full-time homemaker. The concern here is for the needs of the traditional nuclear family—the two-parent family willing to forgo the immediate financial benefits of a second earner in favor of a balanced domestic life in which more resources are invested in child rearing and family relationships. In 1977 approximately 27% of husband–wife families appeared to fit this pattern. It is difficult to predict how many additional families would adopt this pattern if the costs of electing to be a full-time homemaker were reduced.

The sacrifice of status and money, to put it bluntly, forms the most significant cost for full-time homemaker families. It has been suggested that the status and value of homemaker services will increase as these activities become increasingly scarce.[37] Rather than awaiting the homemaker's near extinction to herald her worth, it is possible to design family-oriented policies that offer normative recognition and support for domestic activities and child-rearing functions. The White House Conference on Families made a token nod in this direction with three recommendations addressed explicitly to homemakers. Two of those recommendations call for government to classify homemaking as a career and to institute a National Homemakers Week. These are airy symbolic gestures that in an earlier time, perhaps, would have confirmed the homemakers' venerable status. However, they lack the social and economic force to bestow that status or to reverse the decline it has experienced in recent years.

Beyond these symbolic motions, the White House Conference on Families also recommended that additional tax credits or exemptions be allowed for full-time homemakers. While this recommendation offers a substantive response to the economic needs of full-time homemaker families, it depicts a static view of full-time homemaker services and advances a simplistic solution to the long-term costs of this family arrangement. The contributions and value of full-time homemakers to their families and to society vary according to different stages of the family life cycle.

When families were larger and life was not quite so long, the duties of housewife and mother constituted a lifelong occupation. Technological advancements in family planning have made it possible to control both the number of children and the timing of their arrival. Washing machines, self-cleaning ovens, wash-and-wear fabrics, vacuum cleaners, dishwashers, and other modern devices have lightened household chores. Today, there is on the average probably a 15-to-20-year period of family life during which the combined duties of housework and child rearing can command a homemaker's full time and energy without invoking Parkinson's law.

During the 15-to-20-year period that a full-time homemaker is engaged in raising children and maintaining the household, her family accepts a lower level of material consumption in exchange for more personalized care and home-centered activities that induce greater parent–child interaction than that experienced in a family without a full-time homemaker.[38] Assuming that a family is not impoverished to start with, the choice between higher levels of material consumption and a more traditional domestic life is largely a matter of value preferences. As family incomes approach the poverty level, economic considerations gain weight. But for the vast majority of families above the poverty level it is not a purely economic decision. Over the child-rearing period trade-offs between costs and benefits of a full-time homemaker involve qualitative dimensions of family life that are difficult to price.

However, beyond this 15-to-20-year period the costs become more evident. As children grow up and leave, the homemaker's economic contribution to the family depreciates. As the job of child rearing is completed, the daily satisfactions and social status of motherhood begin to wane. At the same time, there is also a decline in the homemaker's prospects of gaining new status and expanding economic opportunities through employment outside the home. With no paid work experience or at best an erratic record and a diploma that is more than 15 years old, the career options for middle-aged homemakers entering the labor market are highly restricted. At this juncture full-time homemakers begin to pay the heaviest price for electing their style of family life.

It is at this point in the family life cycle that a policy to compensate families for the presence of full-time homemakers can do the most good. The basic mechanism of such a policy would be a "social credit" awarded by the federal government for each year a full-time housekeeper remains at home with children who are under 17 years of age. The amount of credit could vary according to the number of children, let us say up to three children. In that case, at the maximum a full-time housekeeper could earn 48 units of social credit. Variations on this scheme could include providing social credits to housekeepers who care for disabled parents and giving additional weight to home care for children with special problems. Both men and women who were full-time housekeepers would qualify for these credits. Each unit of social credit could be exchanged for either: (a) tuition for four units of undergraduate academic training, (b) tuition for three units of technical school training, (c) tuition for two units of graduate education, or (d) an award of ¼ of a preference point on federal civil service examinations. In spirit, this scheme is akin to veterans' benefits, which are granted in recognition of people who sacrificed career opportunities while serving the nation. The home-maker's contribution to national well-being is obviously quite different from that of veterans. The time and effort invested in domestic labor and child rearing powerfully influence the values, health, and behavior of the nation's youth—shaping the moral, physical, and intellectual stock of its future citizens.

There are, of course, many details of this scheme that would need to be worked out. It would be a costly policy, though not necessarily more expensive than schemes for children's allowances or universal provision of subsidized day-care centers, neither of which lends direct support or social sanction to the full-time homemaker. In response to some of the criticisms of universal allocations (discussed in chap. 4), an element of selectivity could be introduced into the social credit scheme by treating the cash value of benefits exchanged for tuition as taxable income. This policy would allow social credits to remain universal at the point of distribution but become selective at the point of consumption, with families in the upper income brackets returning most of the benefits in taxes.

The family social credit scheme will not solve the problems of poverty, which are addressed by many proposals under the mantle of family policy. That problem is another matter, one properly handled through reform of income maintenance programs. What this approach to family policy does offer is public affirmation and practical support for the values of parenthood and traditional family life. It invests the role of unpaid domestic labor with formal status and social benefits that encourage household activity during the period of family life that it is most needed and most rewarding. It also facilitates the transition from unpaid domestic labor to paid employment at the point of diminishing returns in the full-time homemaker's social and economic contribution to family life.

For women who want a balanced family life and a full-time career, a family credit scheme would open a successive route along which both are possible. Because this route encompasses a 25-to-30-year period of employment, it may close off a few career options which require early training and many years of preparation. There must be some price for enjoying the choice of two callings in life. This is a different path from the continuous paid career line that men typically follow. It may be better.

Certainly, without some sort of public intervention in support of domesticity there is little reason to anticipate an increase in the American family's capacity to provide informal care to its dependent members and others in the community. Full-time homemakers represent the staple fabric of informal social support networks. Their time and energy contribute to the resiliency of these systems of voluntary aid, a resiliency that is being firmly tested in the emerging framework of welfare capitalism.

NOTES

1. Joseph A. Schumpeter, *Capitalism, Socialism and Democracy*, 3d ed. (New York: Harper & Row, 1950), p. 160.

2. Harold Wilensky and Charles Lebeaux, *Industrial Society and Social Welfare* (New York: Russell Sage Foundation, 1958), pp. 72–73; Charles Wolf, Jr., "Institutions and Economic Development," *American Economic Review*, 45 (Dec. 1955), 872–73.

3. E. Wayne Nafizger, "The Effect of the Nigerian Extended Family on Entrepreneurial Activity," *Economic Development and Cultural Change*, 18 (Oct. 1969), 25–33.

4. E. Anthony Wrigley, "Reflections on the History of the Family," *Daedalus*, 106 (Spring 1977), 71–85.

5. Daniel Bell, *The Cultural Contradictions of Capitalism* (New York: Basic Books, 1976), p. 21.

6. Robert Heilbroner, "The Demand for the Supply Side," *New York Review of Books* (June 11, 1981), p. 41.

7. Carolyn Edwards, *USDA Estimates of the Cost of Raising a Child: A Guide to their Use and Interpretation*, U.S. Department of Agriculture, Miscellaneous Publication 1411, p. 47.

8. Schumpeter, *Capitalism*, p. 158.

9. George Gilder, *Wealth and Poverty* (New York: Basic Books, 1981), p. 69.

10. Alan Carlson, "Families, Sex and the Liberal Agenda," *Public Interest*, 50 (Winter 1980), 62–79.

11. For further discussion of this problem, see Nathan Glazer, "The Limits of Social Policy," *Commentary*, 52 (Sept. 1971), 51–58, and the cogent empirical analyses in Robert Moroney, *The Family and the State* (London: Longman, 1976).

12. Clair Vickery, "Women's Economic Contribution to the Family," in *The Subtle Revolution/Women at Work*, ed. Ralph Smith (Washington, D.C.: Urban Institute Press, 1979), p. 184.

13. Some of these costs will be reduced as the Reagan administration's 1981 tax reform eases the so-called marriage penalty on income earned by two-paycheck families.

14. For additional discussion of this issue see Vickery, "Women's Economic Contribution," pp. 162–64.

15. The $9,410 estimate is based on figures in Wendyce Brody, "Economic Value of a Housewife," *Research and Statistics Note*, U.S. Dept. of Health, Education and Welfare, Office of Research and Statistics Note no. 9, Aug. 28, 1975, which I adjusted for inflation;

the $12,000 estimate is made by Gilder, *Wealth and Poverty*, p. 15, adjusting for inflation and using data from Scott Burns, *Home Inc.: The Hidden Wealth and Power of the American Household* (New York: Doubleday, 1975), pp. 16–28.

16. Findings are from Kathryn E. Walker and Margaret Woods, *Time Use: A Measure of Household Production of Family Goods and Services*, American Home Economics Association, 1976, cited in Vickery, "Women's Economic Contribution," pp. 188–92.

17. Phillips Cutright, "Income and Family Events: Marital Stability," *Journal of Marriage and the Family*, 33 (May 1971), 291–306.

18. William J. Goode, "Marital Satisfaction and Instability: A Cross Cultural Analysis of Divorce Rates," *International Social Science Journal*, 5 (1962), 507–26.

19. Michael T. Hannan, Nancy Brandon Tuma, and Lyle Groeneveld, "Income and Marital Events: Evidence From an Income Maintenance Experiment," *American Journal of Sociology*, 82 (May 1977), 1186–211.

20. Similar results were found for a smaller sample in the New Jersey and Scranton, Pennsylvania, income maintenance experiments. See Jon Knudsen, Robert Scott, and Arnold Shore, "Changes in Household Composition," in *Final Report of the New Jersey Graduated Work Incentive Program*, ed. Harold Watts and Albert Ress (Madison: University of Wisconsin Institute for Research on Poverty, 1974), vol. 3, part D, pp. 1–41.

21. Some of the reasons for these discrepant findings are analyzed in Hannan, Tuma, and Groeneveld, "Income and Marital Events"; see also Maurice MacDonald and Isabel V. Sawhill, "Welfare Policy and the Family," *Public Policy*, 26 (Winter 1978), 107–19.

22. The short-term versus long-term effects of SIME/DIME on marital stability are discussed in James W. Albrecht, "Negative Income Taxation and Divorce in SIME/DIME," *Journal of the Institute for Socioeconomic Studies*, 4 (Autumn 1979), 75–82.

23. Alice S. Rossi, "A Biosocial Perspective on Parenting," *Daedalus*, 106 (Spring 1977), 13.

24. B. E. Cogswell, "Variant Family Forms and Lifestyles: Rejection of the Traditional Nuclear Family," *Family Coordinator*, 24: 4 (1975), 401.

25. President Jimmy Carter, "Statement Announcing the White House Conference on Families," U.S. Office of the White House Press Secretary, Jan. 30, 1978.

26. Constance Ahrons, "Redefining the Divorced Family: A Conceptual Framework," *Social Work*, 25 (Nov. 1980), 437.

27. For an eloquent statement of the traditional perspective, see Michael Novak, "The Family Out of Favor," *Harper's* (Apr. 1976), pp. 37–46.

28. White House Conference on Families, *Listening to America's Families: Action for the 80's*, Summary of the Report to the President, Congress and Families of the Nation (Washington, D.C.: U.S. GPO, 1980), pp. 16–17.

29. For a review of approaches to family policy in Austria, Czechoslovakia, France, and other nations see Sheila Kamerman and Alfred Kahn, eds., *Family Policy: Government and Families in Fourteen Countries* (New York: Columbia University Press, 1978).

30. White House Conference, *Listening to America's Families*, p. 37.

31. Ibid., p. 22.

32. William Sonnenstuhl and James E. O'Donnell, "EAPs: The Why's and How's of Planning Them," *Personnel Administrator* (Nov. 1980), pp. 35–38.

33. James T. Wrich, *The Employee Assistance Program*, rev. ed. (Center City, Minn.: Hazelden, 1980).

34. Carlson, "Families," p. 72.

35. Gallup Organization, "American Families—1980," report submitted to the White House Conference on Families, June 5, 1980, by the Gallup Organization, Inc., Princeton, N.J.

36. U.S. Dept. of Health and Human Services, Administration for Children, Youth and Families, *The Status of Children, Youth, & Families, 1979* (Washington, D.C.: U.S. GPO, 1980), p. 132.

37. Muriel Nissel, "The Family and the Welfare State," *New Society*, 56 (Aug. 7, 1980), 259–62.

38. Vickery, "Women's Economic Contribution," pp. 189–92.

SIX

THE RESILIENCY OF VOLUNTARY AID

Self-help and voluntarism evoke visions of individual effort, family care, neighborliness, community support, and collective action. Because these ideas encompass such a broad range of social activities, conservatives, liberals, and radicals alike subscribe to self-help and voluntarism with varying expectations. Conservatives advocate voluntary activity in the social market as a substitute for government intervention. Liberals see voluntary aid as a way to supplement and extend services in the social market.

Both liberals and conservatives are attracted to voluntarism as a device for sustaining social structures that mediate between the individual and the state. In this broad sense voluntarism provides the impetus for religious, ethnic, neighborhood, and other types of associative communities that nurture the pluralistic culture of American democracy. Although they agree on the general value of associative communities, liberals and conservatives differ somewhat about the more precise purposes of these mediating structures. Conservatives lean toward the defensive view of mediating structures as mechanisms that protect the individual against the bureaucratic excesses of central government. Liberals endorse a more aggressive stance, whereby the role of mediating structures is to convey collective demands for social welfare benefits and reform. Radicals are similarly drawn to the possibilities of voluntarism as a vehicle of collective action but for higher stakes than liberal reform. In the radical view, voluntary associations are building blocks for a large community of interests organized around social class and aimed at advancing the cause of socialism.

In expressing these alternative views of self-help and voluntarism, the language of "empowerment" is used to embellish conservative, liberal, and radical positions. Conservatives support the idea that people should be empowered to help themselves through informal arrangements at the local level. Liberals agree but go a step further, recommending that individuals should also be empowered to bargain for their proper share of public benefits. Mediating structures are seen as the means for channeling individual claims on the social market into group interests that demand attention in the political arena. For radicals, "empowerment" means to gain the balance of power necessary to alter the basic structure of social and economic relationships in society.

The social market may be divided into a public and a voluntary sector, between which there is, of course, a large gray area of nongovernmental voluntary agencies financed in varying degrees by public funds. In the voluntary sector the emphasis on different interpretations of self-help shifts with the tides of liberal and conservative influence. Beyond a few brief and scattered episodes, radical ideas have had little practical impact on the development of the voluntary sector.

Between 1960 and the late 1970s prevailing conceptions of self-help were shaped by liberal thought, which promoted collective and formal approaches. The citizen participation requirements of the Economic Opportunity Act of 1964, the Older Americans Act of 1965, the Title XX amendments of 1974, and almost every other piece of social legislation during this period provided a broad statutory base for self-help through collective action. Groups organized around neighborhoods, ethnic status, age cohort, and common service needs were encouraged to represent their interests in state and local planning for the allocation of social benefits. At the same time, the introduction of purchase-of-service arrangements between public and voluntary agencies (discussed in chap. 1) led to the expansion of formally organized voluntary services in that gray area between the public and voluntary sectors of the social market. These two approaches to self-help that distinguished voluntary activity in the 1960s and 1970s have one important feature in common. Both collective action through citizen participation and the delivery of services through formal organizations are closely affiliated with and often financially dependent upon the public sector of the social market.

In contrast the conservative position on voluntary aid turns away from the public sector toward individual and informal paths to self-help. These approaches emphasize the mobilization of familial and neighborhood support networks to provide social care and assistance; they encourage private donations of time and money to support local services delivered under voluntary auspices; and they invite interest groups to contribute to social welfare activities through the creative use of their own resources. It is along these avenues that conservative exhortations to invigorate the American tradition of self-help have accompanied the contraction of public financing for social welfare programs in the early 1980s. The liberal response to this retrenchment calls for converting the "self-help movement into an ally of those who are fighting for the expansion and reorganization of Federal programs in health, mental health, schools, and elsewhere."[1]

While the voluntary sector is being asked to compensate for the reduction of public provisions in the social market, the type of voluntary aid needed and its capacity to respond to this appeal are unclear. There are at least four modes of self-help in the voluntary sector: (1) informal care provided spontaneously by relatives and friends, (2) supportive services provided by neighborhood volunteers working through local agencies, (3) mutual aid provided by groups whose members share interests in a particular need for service or a common cause for social action, and (4) basic professional services provided by formal voluntary organizations.[2] To assess the resiliency of voluntary action in the social market, one must consider the various demands and opportunities associated with these alternative forms of self-help.

INFORMAL CARE: WHERE SELF-HELP BEGINS

Self-help begins at home. The family is the most intimate and natural arrangement for providing informal care to its dependent members. In recent times several social and demographic trends have had a significant impact on the demand for and the supply of family care resources.

While filial responsibility is an ancient duty, the full force of this moral contract has never been stronger or more pervasive than in recent decades. This development reflects, in part, the simple fact that there are more elderly parents about to claim their end of the bargain. Average life expectancy has increased from 47 years in 1900 to 74 years in 1979. Over the same period the percentage of older persons almost tripled from 4 to 11% of the population. Among the elderly the greatest need for care is experienced by the group over 75 years of age, which is rapidly increasing. Estimates indicate that by the year 2000 the number of elderly 75 to 84 years of age is expected to rise by 57%, and the ranks of those aged 85 years and over are expected to double.[3] Moreover, in the shift from an agricultural to an industrial society the elderly lost a considerable degree of economic control over family affairs which they had exercised on the farm. As a farmer, the aging parent could change his pattern of activity and rely more upon adult children for heavy work. It is difficult to discern whether, when parents owned the farm, their children's assistance stemmed from a sense of moral obligation or from the economic interdependence of the family unit. "It is only," as Schorr observes, "when an economy that separated wages from ownership meant that the old person was no longer in control, that many adult children had reason to examine their willingness to help their parents."[4]

Along with extending the average life span, scientific advances have boosted the survival rates of severely handicapped children. This increasing number of physically and mentally disabled children is another source of the intensified demand on the caretaking resources of families in modern times.

While the growing numbers of frail elderly and severely handicapped children have heightened the demand on families to care for dependent members, the supply of potential caretakers to meet this demand has been dwindling. Owing to changes in family size, marriage rates, and female participation in the labor force, fewer women are available to perform their traditional function of providing informal care in family life. In the United States household size has decreased from an average of 4.11 in 1930 to 2.86 in 1980. Eversley's estimates illustrate the impact of a similar decline upon the number of female relatives on hand to care for the dependent elderly in Britain. According to his figures, by the time a typical British couple married in 1950 reach their eighties they would have 11 surviving female relatives, 3 of whom would not be in paid employment and available as potential caretakers. In contrast, the typical couple married in 1920 and now in their eighties has 42 female relatives, 14 of whom are not employed.[5] Changing marriage and divorce rates have also reduced the pool of potential caretakers. Higher marriage rates have decreased the number of "maiden aunts" who in the past often assumed major responsibilities for informal family care.[6] Higher divorce rates have swelled the ranks of single parents for whom the struggle to raise children and meet living expenses leaves little to draw upon for other caretaking functions.

The detrimental effects of smaller family size and changing patterns of marriage on the kinship network's potential to provide informal care are compounded by the steady rise of female participation in the labor force. In the United States the proportion of working-age women in the labor force in recent decades has almost doubled, rising from 27% in 1940 to 51% in 1980. Three-fourths of these women work full time. Women at work obviously have less time and energy to invest in child-rearing responsibilities (discussed in chap. 5) as well as in tending to the needs of elderly and disabled relatives.

Despite the declining supply of potential caretakers, the traditional obligations of kinship aid have not been abandoned. On the contrary, there is considerable evidence that families provide a major portion of social care and support for the elderly and disabled.[7] The level of contact between the elderly and their adult children has remained stable and fairly high. Nationwide surveys in 1957 and 1975 report that almost 80% of elderly parents saw at least one of their children the week before they were interviewed.[8] It appears that a good deal of assistance is furnished in these relationships. According to estimates from the National Center for Health Statistics as much as 80% of the home health care services for the elderly are provided by family members.[9] A similar pattern of familial support is found in Britain, where 36% of the handicapped elderly and 50% of the severely handicapped elderly lived with their adult children.[10] Family care for substantially retarded children is also widespread. In the United States 67% and in Britain 70% of severely mentally handicapped children live at home with their parents.[11]

The many families that assume a heavy share of the responsibility for tending to the needs of severely dependent members do so at great cost. The financial hardships, marital disruptions, physical fatigue, and social adversities involved in caring for retarded children and disabled elderly are well documented.[12] But one does not need much empirical evidence to recognize that the strains of raising a mentally retarded child are staggering and relentless. Virtually every facet of family life is affected as the daily pressures of coping with a handicapped child embrace career patterns, recreational activities, friendship patterns, housing choices, and marital relations. These pressures are intensified by the high degree of social isolation typically experienced by families with retarded children.[13] Caring for the disabled elderly begets similar hardships, though usually of a shorter duration, which holds out the prospect of caretakers resuming a less harrowing existence at some future point in their lives.

The increasing scale of social dependency, the diminishing supply of family caretakers, and the high personal costs associated with this function are dubious testimony to the hopes that informal kinship supports will expand to compensate for the reduction of public services. As in the past, the burdens of familial care in the foreseeable future will rest mainly on women, whose continued performance in these roles, as Parker suggests, cannot be taken for granted.[14] If the family's capacity to serve dependent elderly and handicapped members has not already been stretched to its limit, there is probably little more than a trace of slack remaining in the realm of informal care. Thus, exhortations to extend the contributions of informal care to the voluntary sector of the social market in the 1980s are unlikely to produce a significant advance in this area.

There is, however, another area of voluntary support in which the discharge of familial obligation has substantial room for improvement. Several social welfare policy analysts have observed that high divorce rates may not necessarily result in a diminishing supply of family caretakers. It is possible, they note, that through divorce and remarriage these units will eventually forge extensive kinship networks in which natural parents are joined by step parents and grandparents to provide a broader base of informal supports for children and the elderly.[15] While it is encouraging to contemplate such a rejuvenation of familial solidarity, the modern consequences of divorce, separation, and out-of-wedlock births in American families point very sharply in another direction.

The growing rates of divorce, separation, and out-of-wedlock births between 1970 and 1980 have produced a 69% increase in single-parent families during this period. In 1980 close to 18% of families with children were single-parent families.[16] According to current trends, by 1990 one-third of all children are likely to live with a divorced parent at some time before their eighteenth birthday. This proportion increases to 50% when including single-parent families in which the mother was never married, was widowed, or was separated.[17]

Single-parent families, 90% of whom are maintained by women, have received meager economic assistance from the absent father. Indeed, Census Bureau figures reveal that only 34.6% of single-parent families headed by women receive any child support payments from the father.[18] For those who do contribute to their children's financial support the average amount is approximately $2,000, or about what it would cost to place one child in a day-care center if the mother worked full time.[19]

Although the Child Support Enforcement Program was enacted in 1975 under Title IV-D of the Social Security Act, the major focus of this legislation is upon female recipients of public assistance (AFDC). Economically marginal female-headed households and single-parents from the middle class who suffer a serious decline in their standard of living when financially abandoned are usually left to their own limited resources. And even with the Child Support Enforcement Program, AFDC recipients gain little additional support. In 1977 the courts and other legal agencies awarded child-care support to 29% of AFDC recipients. Only 13% of these cases, however, eventually obtained any payment from the absent parent.[20]

There are various reasons why absent fathers contribute so little to the support of their children. The adversarial atmosphere of many divorces and separations is hardly conducive to generous impulses. The absence of normative standards of what constitutes a fair amount of child support lends a high degree of uncertainty and much scope for disagreement on this matter. And, no doubt, some of the fathers are just economically unable to provide financial assistance. The economic relationship of divided families is a complex and highly sensitive area for public policy and regulation. Child Support Enforcement programs often have difficulty locating fathers, then flounder in the family courts, and finally, obtaining a court-ordered support payment, are frequently incapable of enforcing collection.[21] But whatever the explanations for low rates of child support, the behavior of many absent fathers simply does not bring to mind a powerful and lasting sense of paternal obligation once the family unit is physically divided. What this phenomenon does reveal are a fragile link in kinship support networks and the vulnerability of informal care to the rising levels of family dissolution.

FROM GOOD NEIGHBORS TO PAID VOLUNTEERS

Although family units are the core of informal support networks, these structures include friends and good neighbors as well. Gans's study in the late 1950s described how good neighbors contributed to social care among the "urban villagers" of Boston's West End. He found, for example, one mother "who functioned as a 'visiting nurse' on an informal and unpaid basis, took care of neighborhood families if one of the adults were ill or in the hospital." Caretaking roles of this sort, Gans suggests, "are not distinctive to the West End and can probably be found in all communities."[22] Similar social care activities were reported in Young and Willmott's study of London's East End in the 1950s, where an open door and a pot of tea brewing on the burner symbolized the availability of spontaneous neighborly aid.[23]

Since these studies in the late 1950s, social patterns of neighbor-hood life have been changing, just as urban renewal has altered the physical character of many communities. It is impossible to trace how local support networks may have evolved among the working-class urban villagers in Boston's West End, as this neighborhood was demolished in the 1960s to make way for urban renewal. In the process of redevelopment most of the original residents and businesses were displaced. London's East End has also undergone physical changes but not quite so drastic. Here, recent efforts to follow up earlier findings on informal social care networks reveal a significant deterioration, if not collapse, of the old-style neighborly support systems.[24]

The full extent of good neighborly aid is difficult to gauge. Not only is the evidence on neighborly support scattered and inconclusive, but this activity can take many forms. Numerous instances of neighborly support can be cited by those who extol the contributions of such assistance and the potential to draw increasing aid from these quarters. No doubt many good neighbors are around to lend an occasional hand baby-sitting, to pick up some food at the grocery, and to offer advice on various problems.[25] Whether they are available in any significant number to assist on a sustained basis with unpleasant problems of those nearby who may be confused, disabled, incontinent, mentally retarded, or delinquent is entirely another matter. It is a matter of some consequence, however, as informal social care often requires a sustained effort dealing with human needs much more demanding than those that might be satisfied by a few words of advice and good cheer over a cup of coffee. The question of how many local caretakers may be willing to offer informal help cannot be answered, as Parker observes, without considering the duration, intensity, and complexity of the care requested in specific circumstances, as well as the prognosis of the person needing this care.[26]

Although decisive evidence on the depth of neighborly aid is unavailable, there are reasons to believe that it constitutes a shallow reservoir of social support best suited for temporary help on simple problems. As previously noted, the pool of married women who traditionally supplied most of the informal neighborhood care is shrinking. Those available are likely to give first priority to the growing needs for aid among their elderly relatives. In addition, the provision of informal care by friends and neighbors rests on somewhat different considerations from the traditional sense of social duty and emotional ties of kinship that underlie familial obligations to support dependent members. In the absence of kinship ties, altruistic sentiments and anticipation of reciprocity loom larger in social care arrangements among friends and neighbors than in family circles. The likelihood of receiving aid in return for services provided to neighbors over an extended period of time depends in part on the stability of the helping network. It is easy to imagine how one's confidence in the reciprocity of neighborly support networks might be tempered by the transient quality of modern community life. Between 1975 and 1980 approximately 45% of the population had changed their place of residence.[27] In modern times, the kind of social cohesion that encourages the development of strong reciprocal bonds is seriously threatened by the combined effects of high residential mobility, rising divorce rates, and the decline of local integrative institutions, such as the neighborhood school, which served as an incubator for expressions of common interest and commitments to community functions.

One way to shore up informal support by neighborhood caretakers is to institutionalize these activities, placing them under the auspices of social welfare agencies. Providing a more formal structure for the transaction of voluntary assistance endows these services with a degree of stability, but it does not solve the initial issue of how to increase the number of volunteers with the time and inclination to perform local caretaking duties on a sustained basis. Over the last decade the British have approached this issue by offering limited financial remuneration to volunteers. Numerous good neighbor schemes have been developed, such as those in Kent and Liverpool, which employ "paid volunteers" to care for the elderly.[28] The payment for these services is minimal, usually between the equivalent of $500 and $600 a year in addition to travel costs. In the Liverpool project, volunteers agree to work a minimum of fifteen hours per week. This is a relatively high number of hours compared to typical voluntary experiences in the United States, where fewer than 7% of all the people identified in some form of volunteer work in 1975 averaged 6 hours or more of service per week.[29] Despite the relatively high investment of time required in the Liverpool project, applicants to work in this good neighbor program apparently exceeded the number of positions available. Project organizers report, on the one hand, that payments do not interfere with the informal neighborly character of services and, on the other hand, that they add to the quality and reliability of volunteer work.

Higher payments are offered for certain other voluntary activities previously performed without remuneration. In Kent a scheme to recruit foster parents for disturbed adolescent children, for example, pays a stipend equivalent to approximately $4,000 a year in addition to the normal payment for room and board.[30] In the United States, a different type of program using paid volunteers in the area of foster care was established under the Domestic Volunteer Act of 1973. The Foster Grandparent Program is open only to elderly participants, providing them stipends to serve children in day-care centers, institutions, and their own homes. The elderly may earn up to approximately $1,700 a year working a maximum of 20 hours a week in this program.[31]

These examples of paid volunteer programs in Britain and the United States represent a method to strengthen informal social care that is gaining in popularity.[32] It is reasonable to assume that the introduction of modest economic incentives into the sphere of informal voluntary assistance will enhance the reliability and availability of voluntary workers. Against these presumed advantages, however, one must weigh several other possible consequences.

The essential character of informal voluntary aid rests on a blend of personal sympathies, altruistic sentiments, and reciprocal expectations. These are the "natural" inducements that join givers and receivers in the spontaneous social transactions of neighborly assistance. It is, of course, conceivable that natural inducements may be reinforced by a dash of economic reward. Yet at some point, concrete economic incentives to provide social care will override the more ethereal inducements of sympathy, sentiment, and expectation. It is difficult to know for specific individuals the extent to which payments of varying size transform what were originally social transactions into primarily economic transactions. In the examples given, the $500 for good neighbors, $1,700 for foster grandparents, and $4,000 for foster parents are sums that range from somewhat more than a symbolic gesture to an amount that might well be considered low paid employment.

It is also difficult to gauge the effects that a shift toward economic transactions ultimately might have on informal helping relationships. At the same time that a paid volunteer's work assumes the quality of an economic transaction, it takes on the complexion of cheap labor being exploited under the moral credibility of voluntarism. A sense of exploitation would surely create a hard edge in the relationship between caretakers and clients. Finally, there is the issue of whether paid volunteers would eventually drive unpaid volunteers from the ranks of informal caretakers. To put it another way: How many local caretakers would be expected to volunteer to do work for free that other members of the community are being paid for by public and private agencies?

The potential for economic incentives to undermine the intrinsic merits of informal voluntary aid suggests that policies along these lines should be drawn very delicately. The level of payment is a crucial consideration. If kept low enough to represent symbolic compensation, stipends can make the voluntary effort somewhat more rewarding in terms of both economic and social recognition for the work performed without recasting it as paid employment. But symbolic payments may not be enough to sustain voluntary efforts that require long and hard work.

An alternative approach to strengthening good neighborly assistance involves reducing the burdens of social care. Programs that decrease the pressures on local caretakers would allow informal support to flourish under the conditions most conducive to this type of aid. While most good neighbors cannot provide extensive care for a physically disabled or otherwise dependent friend, many might be able to offer supplemental forms of help, such as transportation to and from an adult day-care facility several times a week. A broad infrastructure of formal services in the public sector of the social market would allow, perhaps encourage, good neighbors to contribute useful help within the practical limits of their own resources. The notion of indirectly bracing informal social supports by enlarging the provision of formal services in the public sector, however, contradicts the prevailing conservative view that informal care can be extended to compensate for part of the reductions in public social services.

MUTUAL AID: SERVICE AND ACTION

Groups organized for purposes of mutual aid invest the fabric of American life with considerable strength and flexibility. These groups are composed of peers joined by a common problem which the group is committed to solve or mitigate. Estimated at between several hundred thousand and half a million in number, mutual aid groups deal with such diverse problems as alcoholism, drug abuse, bereavement, smoking, obesity, depression, loneliness, and all sorts of social and physical handicaps.[33] The myriad functions performed through mutual aid have been categorized along several dimensions. The most common distinction is between groups devoted to guidance/supportive services and those engaged in social action, although many groups carry out both types of activities. Groups providing guidance and supportive services are further delineated according to purposes such as coping with stress, changing behavior, and self-actualization.[34]

Among mutual aid groups involved in social action, some focus upon the reform of private enterprise, but most are concerned with changing public policies and increasing the allocation of benefits through the social market. The environment for social action in the public sector has undergone a significant change since the early 1960s, when President Johnson's Great Society programs stimulated the formation of thousands of citizen groups organized around local issues in the allocation of social welfare resources. As the social market continued to expand from the 1960s through the mid-1970s the claims of different groups could be settled through compromises under which everyone gained. In the early 1980s the contraction of social welfare expenditures has created a more troublesome environment for social action. As social welfare resources decline, the competition among groups comes to resemble a zero-sum game in which one group's gain is another's loss.

How will voluntary groups oriented toward social action respond to this changing environment? One scenario envisions a powerful coalition of self-help groups gathered to launch a collective struggle against the reduction in public expenditures for social welfare.[35] Another view suggests that groups exercising what Glennerster calls "consumer rationality" will seek to hold on to what they have, resisting cuts in programs that affect their immediate interests.[36] If consumer rationality prevails, social action is likely to become a more abrasive process marked by heightened conflict among local voluntary groups.

Whereas liberals hope that through social action mutual aid groups can reverse the decline of public support for social welfare, conservatives recommend strengthening the service functions of these voluntary groups to supplant public provisions. In assessing the extent to which the benefits of mutual aid groups can replace those of public social services one must recognize that a large portion of these groups are organized around matters of peripheral concern to the welfare state. Raising consciousness, losing weight, finding a mate, and weaning the young are normal trials of living that may benefit from mutual aid; they do not, however, impact upon the focal problems of public policy.[37]

Leaving aside the varied efforts in pursuit of happiness and self-improvement, there remains a significant number of mutual aid groups supplying services that are central to the affairs of the welfare state. Policies to strengthen these services must come to grips with two basic issues. First is the question of who gets served through mutual aid. The answer wavers in the direction of the middle class. For a body of strangers to create an association and provide one another with ongoing social and psychological supports requires the kinds of organizational and interpersonal skills possessed more frequently by middle-class people than by the poor. Indeed there is some empirical evidence suggesting that the most disadvantaged segments of the population are least likely to form and benefit from mutual aid groups.[38] There are, nevertheless, vivid examples of drug addicts, ex-prisoners, and other highly disadvantaged groups which organize and sustain mutual aid efforts. Synanon, the Delancey Street Foundation, and the Black Muslims, for instance, are cases in point.

Several conditions apparently facilitate mutual aid among disadvantaged groups. As Durman points out, one set of conducive circumstances involves strict discipline and firm leadership operating within an ideological framework that is often "anti-establishment."[39] Under these authoritarian circumstances group members benefit from mutual aid at a significant cost to personal independence and identity. Although the high degree of social control in these groups creates a firm bond of membership, it is not without potential for great harm; the mass suicide at Jonestown is chilling testimony to this darker side of self-help.

The second question is: What systematic efforts might public policies feasibly initiate to strengthen provisions of service through mutual aid? Here the prescriptions are thin. There is general agreement about the value of educational campaigns to inform professionals and the lay public about the importance of mutual aid and the range of self-help groups operating in local communities. There is also agreement that professional assistance and the resources of established social services should be accessible to mutual aid groups that may want to draw upon help from these quarters, with the caveat that professional intervention be limited to no more than a supplementary role in mutual aid activities.[40] Beyond these orthodox recommendations, a few suggestions have been put forth advising legal recognition, direct financial support of mutual aid groups, and the establishment of a federal task force and White House Conferences to study, plan, and coordinate policy incentives in this area.[41]

These prescriptions for strengthening mutual aid are vulnerable to criticism on several points. Publicizing, and supplementing mutual aid would no doubt enhance existing groups, including some that are extremely authoritarian and others that may employ irregular, possibly harmful, therapeutic methods. Groups that operate with strict discipline and authoritarian leadership are likely to move more rapidly than others in seizing opportunities for favorable publicity and supplemental resources. In the absence of evidence that a group poses a serious threat to the well-being of its members, there is little ground to discriminate among the various self-help arrangements that deserve to be strengthened. Such evidence is rarely available before the fact of some concrete harm has been accomplished. Public measures for the promotion of mutual aid unqualified by standards of acceptable service thus invite exploitation by groups with visions and methods of an intemperate, if not detrimental, nature. On the other hand the development of standards that might afford legal recognition along with a substantial infusion of direct financial support would transform the social and economic character of mutual aid groups, moving these associations into the orbit of formal nonprofit organizations. Whatever the benefits of such a development, many unique qualities of mutual aid would be lost in the process. These observations suggest an inherent limitation on systematic public efforts to strengthen mutual aid. The problem is that while public policies can do little to arouse the kind of voluntary commitments that are discharged with the spontaneous enthusiasm of mutual aid, they can do much to squelch the primal *esprit de corps* of voluntarism.

ENLARGING THE SCOPE OF FORMAL VOLUNTARY EFFORTS: WHO WILL PAY?

Informal voluntary assistance through kith, kin, and mutual aid provides a vast array of social supports at a nominal cost. There are, however, many serious problems that do not yield to informal aid, requiring instead the knowledge and reliability of professional help. Moreover, some people prefer the privacy and confidentiality of professional services to the public exposure of informal aid. Calls to strengthen the voluntary sector thus include not only informal efforts but also the professional services of formal voluntary organizations. The costs of professional help delivered through the voluntary sector are mainly covered by private contributions and payments for services purchased by public agencies.

Although a boost in private contributions to the voluntary sector could offset some portion of the decline in public expenditures for social welfare, the historic record of charitable giving and projections for the future do not suggest high cause for optimism on this point. United Way campaigns, for example, are a major source of private contributions to voluntary social welfare organizations. Between 1970 and 1980 the increase in funds collected through these campaigns just kept pace with inflation. During this period the base of private charitable support for all voluntary social welfare activities expanded from 2.9 to $4.7 billion, which was well below the rate of inflation.[42]

But even if charitable contributions were regularly on the rise, to enlarge the scope of formal voluntary efforts in the wake of declining public expenditures would require an enormous surge in philanthropic dispensations. Since the early 1960s voluntary organizations have become progressively dependent on purchase-of-service arrangements with government agencies for financial support. This reliance on public funds has climbed so high that by 1980 private contributions accounted for only 33% of the total revenues of voluntary social service, community development, and civic organizations.[43] Given the high degree of dependence on public funds, any decrease in public expenditures for social services would both heighten service demands on voluntary agencies and reduce their fiscal capacity to maintain current levels of effort, let alone to meet the stepped-up demands. Estimates based on proposed federal budget cuts from 1982 through 1985 suggest that the withdrawal of public funds would leave an immense gap to be filled by private contributions for all fields of service in which voluntary agencies are active. If these projected budget cuts were implemented, for example, just to maintain 1980 levels of activity private contributions to voluntary organizations would have to increase by 24% in 1982 and continue increasing each year up to 46% in 1985. This means that each year the rate of private giving would have to multiply from two to four times its highest level of growth since 1960. Going beyond maintenance of effort to fill the entire service gap left by projected cuts in public spending would require that private contributions increase by 60% in 1982, continuing upward to 147% in 1985.[44] These estimates reveal the intense fiscal pressures that are likely to build on formal voluntary activities in the absence of direct support from the public sector of the social market. To alleviate these pressures through private contributions demands a magnitude of charitable giving that has not been seen in modern times.

In sum, formal and informal modes of voluntary action occupy a unique corner of the social market; it is a sector of human dimensions that encourages altruism, charity, and primary group bonding. Although the voluntary sector generates a significant volume of service, there is little evidence that it possesses the inherent capacity to move far beyond current levels of activity or to compensate in any reasonable degree for decreased public spending in the social market. The future of the social market, for better or ill, remains to be shaped by the accomplishments and disappointments of the public sector, which provides the statutory foundation of the welfare state.

NOTES

1. Frank Riessman, "Toward Self-Help," *New York Times*, Mar. 24, 1982, p. 25.

2. Working Party to Review Social Workers' Roles and Tasks, set up by the National Institute of Social Work under the Chairmanship of Peter Barclay, *Social Workers: Their Role and Task* (London: Bedford Square Press, 1982), p. 73.

3. Elaine M. Brody, " 'Women in the Middle' and Family Help to Older People," *Gerontologist*, 21 (Oct. 1981), 472.

4. Alvin Schorr, *Explorations in Social Policy* (New York: Basic Books, 1968), pp. 74-75.

5. D. E. C. Eversley, "Some New Aspects of Ageing in Britain," in *Ageing and the Life Cycle Course in a Cross-Cultural Interdisciplinary Perspective*, ed. T. K. Harevan (New York: Guilford Press, forthcoming), cited in Roy Parker, "Tending and Social Policy," in *A New Look at the Personal Social Services*, ed. E. Matilda Goldberg and Stephen Hatch (London: Policy Studies Institute, Discussion Paper 4, 1981), p. 19.

6. Judith Treas, "Family Support Systems for the Aged," *Gerontologist*, 17 (Dec. 1977), 486-91.

7. See, for example, Ethel Shanas et al., *Old People in Three Industrial Societies* (New York: Atherton, 1968); Lillian Troll, "The Family of Later Life: A Decade Review," *Journal of Marriage and the Family*, 33 (May 1971), 263-90; Brody, "Women in the Middle"; George Brown et al., *Schizophrenia and Social Care* (New York: Oxford University Press, 1966); Steven Segal, "Community Care and Deinstitutionalization: A

Review," *Social Work*, 24 (Nov. 1979), 521–27; and Robert Moroney, *The Family and the State* (London: Longman, 1976).

8. Ethel Shanas, "Social Myth as Hypothesis: The Case of the Family Relations of Old People," *Gerontologist*, 19 (Feb. 1979), 3–9.

9. National Center for Health Statistics, U.S. Dept. of Health, Education and Welfare, "Home Health Care for Persons 55 Years and Over," *Vital and Health Statistics Publication: Statistical Publication Series*, 10, no. 73 (1972).

10. Moroney, *Family and the State*, p. 44.

11. Bonnie Brown Morell, "Deinstitutionalization: Those Left Behind," *Social Work*, 24 (Nov. 1979), 528; Moroney, *Family*, p. 95.

12. See, for example, J. Carr, "The Effect of the Severely Subnormal on Their Families," *Mental Deficiency: The Changing Outlook*, ed. Ann Clarke and Alan Clarke (New York: Free Press, 1975), pp. 807–38; Jacqueline Grad and Peter Sainsbury, "The Effects that Patients Have on Their Families in a Community Care and a Control Psychiatric Service—A Two Year Follow-up," *British Journal of Psychiatry*, 114 (Mar. 1968), 265–78; Moroney, *Family*, pp. 45–46, 70–72; and P. Cohen, "The Impact of the Handicapped Child on the Family," *Social Casework*, 43 (Mar. 1962), 137–42.

13. Moroney, *Family*, pp. 70–71.

14. Parker, "Tending and Social Policy," p. 22.

15. Roger Hadley and Stephen Hatch, *Social Welfare and the Failure of the State* (London: Allen & Unwin, 1981), p. 91; Parker, "Tending and Social Policy," p. 21.

16. U.S. Bureau of Census, *Statistical Abstract of the United States: 1981*, 102d ed. (Washington, D.C.: U.S. GPO, 1981), p. 48.

17. Paul C. Glick, "Children of Divorced Parents in Demographic Perspective," *Journal of Social Issues*, 35: 4 (1979), 176. Another estimate indicates that 50% of all children born in 1980 are likely to spend part of their first 18 years in a female-headed household. See Daniel Patrick Moynihan, "Children and Welfare Reform," *Journal of the Institute for Socioeconomic Studies*, 5 (Spring 1981), 8.

18. U.S. Bureau of Census, *Statistical Abstract*, p. 347.

19. Various estimates of the average child support payment range from $1,800 to $2,430. See Isabel Sawhill, "Developing Normative Standards for Child Support and Alimony Payments" (Washington, D.C.: Urban Institute Press, Apr. 1981), pp. 1–2.

20. Philip Robins and Katherine Dickinson, "Child Support Enforcement," *Journal of the Institute for Socioeconomic Studies*, 7 (Summer 1982), 51–53.

21. For an analysis of the difficulties in implementing the Title IV-D program in New York see Blanche Bernstein, "Shouldn't Low-Income Fathers Support Their Children," *Public Interest*, 66 (Winter 1982), 54–71.

22. Herbert Gans, *The Urban Villagers* (New York: Free Press, 1962), p. 160.

23. Michael Young and Peter Willmott, *Family and Kinship in East London* (London: Routledge & Kegan Paul, 1957).

24. Barry Knight and Ruth Hayes, *Self Help in the Inner City* (London: London Voluntary Service Council, 1981). In this study of four inner London boroughs they found that half the people interviewed did not visit socially with anyone outside their family, let alone engage in neighborly support activities. Many of the respondents did not even know the names of their neighbors.

25. For example, in replicating a 1952 study of community life in Rochester, New York, Albert Hunter found almost 25 years later that there was no decline in the high degree of "informal neighboring," which included activities such as exchanging favors and advice. See Albert Hunter, "The Loss of Community: An Empirical Test," *American Sociological Review*, 40 (Oct. 1975), 537–52.

26. Parker, "Tending and Social Policy," pp. 26–30.

27. U.S. Bureau of Census, *"Statistical Abstract"*, p. 15.

28. These schemes are described in Hadley and Hatch, *Social Welfare*, pp. 137–42.

29. U.S. Bureau of the Census, *Statistical Abstract*, p. 350.

30. Hadley and Hatch, *Social Welfare*, p. 138.

31. Charlane Brown and Mary O'Day, "Services to the Elderly," in *Handbook of the Social Services*, ed. Neil Gilbert and Harry Specht (Englewood Cliffs: Prentice-Hall, 1981), p. 128.

32. In 1975, for example, the American Public Welfare Association advanced the idea of a paid career line for foster parents. See *Standards for Foster Family Service Systems* (Washington, D.C.: American Public Welfare Association, 1975), pp. 43–57. In 1978 the Task Panel on Community Support Systems recommended that the President's Commission on Mental Health adopt a strategy of experimenting with new methods for reimbursement of social support systems which might include direct contracts with mutual help groups (President's Commission on Mental Health, *Task Panel Reports Submitted to the President's Commission on Mental Health*, vol. 2, appendix [Washington, D.C.: U.S. GPO, 1978], pp. 155–156). And Congress has debated a bill proposing cash subsidies to families for providing informal care to their elderly relatives. For an analysis of this bill see Edward Prager, "Subsidized Family Care of the Aged: U.S. Senate Bill 1161," *Policy Analysis*, 4 (Fall 1978), 477–90.

33. The estimates on the number of mutual aid groups come from Alfred Katz and Eugene Bender, "Self-Help Groups in Western Society: History and Prospects, " *Journal of Applied Behavioral Science*, 12: 3 (1976), 278, and President's Commission, *Task Panel Reports*, p. 172.

34. For various typologies of self-help groups see Katz and Bender, "Self-Help Groups," pp. 278–80; Leon Levy, "Self-Help Groups: Types and Psychological Processes," *Journal of Applied Behavioral Science*, 12: 3 (1976), 312–14; and Violet Sieder and Doris Kirshbaum, "Volunteers," *Encyclopedia of Social Work* (Washington, D.C.: National Association of Social Workers, 1977), p. 1587.

35. Riessman, "Toward Self-Help."

36. Howard Glennerster, "Prime Cuts: Public Expenditure and Social Services Planning in a Hostile Environment," *Policy and Politics*, 8: 4 (1980), 367–82.

37. Eugene Durman, "The Role of Self-Help in Service Provision," *Journal of Applied Behavioral Science*, 12: 3 (1976), 333–43.

38. Ibid., pp. 337–38.

39. Ibid. Durman also suggests that intensive involvement by professionals can effect self-help among disadvantaged groups. He notes that a heavy commitment of professional services, however, raises some question about a group's self-help status.

40. Morton Lieberman and Leonard Borman, "Self-Help and Social Research," *Journal of Applied Behavioral Science*, 12: 3 (1976), 461–63.

41. Sol Tax, "Self-Help Groups: Thoughts on Public Policy," *Journal of Applied Behavioral Science*, 12: 3 (1976), 448–54; President's Commission, *Task Panel Reports*, p. 145.

42. U.S. Bureau of the Census, *Statistical Abstract*, pp. 349–50, 458–59.

43. Lester Salamon and Alan Abramson, *The Federal Budget and the Nonprofit Sector* (Washington, D.C.: Urban Institute Press, 1982), p. 18.

44. Ibid., pp. 59–64. These estimates refer to voluntary agencies dealing with a range of activities including social services, community development, civic activities, education, research, health care, culture, and international activities. As the projected budget cuts in the areas of social service and community development are among the highest, the rate of increase in private giving to fill the service gaps in these areas would actually be greater than the figures cited for the entire range of voluntary agencies.

PART IV

THE FUTURE OF WELFARE CAPITALISM

SEVEN

LIMITS OF THE WELFARE STATE

With the boundaries of social and economic markets faintly marked and continually shifting in the currents of social and political change, the dynamic relationship between them is an absorbing feature of welfare capitalism. In the ebb and flow of public support, each market naturally is tempted to press its claims and expand its realm. Earlier we suggested that in their drive to expand the borders of the social market during the 1960s and 1970s liberal proponents failed to recognize several important constraints on the development of a welfare state in a capitalist society. The most fundamental of these constraints involves the fiscal limits of social welfare.

How much social welfare can society afford? And how large an allocation of resources through the social market will a capitalist economy tolerate? In considering these issues one must bear in mind that the welfare state is nonproductive. It may be, as human capital theorists argue, that certain kinds of social welfare provisions are investments in human resources which are conducive to economic growth.[1] But these welfare provisions are created and sustained by surplus produced in the market economy. This dependence on economic surplus places a practical limit on the size of the welfare state. Since the 1960s the American welfare state has been approaching that limit; some might say it has been crossed.

There are different ways to examine the growth of the welfare state. By removing the effects of population growth and inflation, per capita social welfare expenditures in constant prices offer a picture of the social market's expansion which allows us to estimate and compare potential benefits on the individual level over the decades. Under public programs between 1950 and 1960 per capita social welfare expenditures in constant 1978 prices increased by 46% from $405 to $592, as shown in Table 7.1. That increase appears moderate next to the 200% rise from $592 to $1,775 that took place between 1960 and 1978. In current prices per capita social welfare expenditures added up for a family of four crept from 18 to 20% of the median income of

Table 7.1. Per Capita Social Welfare Expenditures, Poverty Threshold, and Median Income

	Per capita social welfare expenditures (constant 1978 prices)	Per capita social welfare expenditures (current prices)	Poverty threshold for four-person family (current prices)	Median family income of all families (current prices)
1950	404.67	152.56	—	3,319
1960	592.16	285.42	3,022	5,620
1970	1,142.13	701.27	3,968	9,867
1978	1,775.23	1,775.23	6,662	17,640

Sources: Data are taken from Alma McMillan and Ann Bixby, "Social Welfare Expenditures, Fiscal Year 1978," *Social Security Bulletin,* 43 (May 1980), Table 2, and U.S. Bureau of the Census, *Statistical Abstract of the United States, 1980* (Washington, D.C.: U.S. GPO), Table 771.

all families between 1950 and 1960, then jumped to 40% of the median family income in 1978.

The poverty index is one yardstick against which to judge the magnitude of per capita social welfare expenditures under public auspices. Measured by this yardstick the figures are rather startling. Per capita social welfare expenditures climbed from 38% of the poverty index for an urban family of four in 1960 to 107% in 1978. Accordingly, if these public expenditures were directly distributed to the *entire population* in the form of cash grants nobody would have fallen below the established poverty line of $6,662 in 1978. For comparisons of this sort one might argue that these figures need some adjusting. At the very least the poverty index excludes the costs of education, which would no longer be available free of charge if public expenditures in this area were transformed into per capita cash grants. Also it might be claimed that the costs of medical care should be treated separately because of the confounding problem that high payments in this area reflect more the presence of severe illness than a material increase in standard of living associated with the reduction of poverty. If payments for all medical care and education in 1978 are subtracted, per capita social welfare expenditures are reduced from 107 to 59% of the poverty index. In this case poverty would be eliminated if the expenditures were distributed not to the entire population but among everyone with incomes below the 1978 national median of $17,640. Indeed, in either of these hypothetical cases a substantial amount of money would go to people who had incomes above the poverty level in the first place.

In drawing the unavoidable conclusion that a fair portion of social market expenditures goes directly into the pockets of middle-class service providers and middle-class recipients, particularly the elderly, we should be careful not to underestimate the extent to which the social market aids the poor. It is difficult to gauge the number of pretransfer poor families lifted out of poverty by the receipt of social welfare benefits. One estimate suggests that if we reversed the flow of social welfare expenditures and subtracted the dollar value of cash and in-kind transfers from the income of those receiving these benefits, the proportion of people below the poverty level would have been 22% in 1980.[2] This figure represents about a 70% increase in the official poverty rate for that year.

Social welfare expenditures clearly account for a significant reduction in the rate of poverty. It is equally clear, however, that a good deal more money is distributed in the social market than would be required to eliminate poverty if payments for the array of existing public provisions were converted to individual cash grants for only low-income people. This straightforward and seemingly simple approach to eliminating poverty has several inviting features: it would offer firm guidelines to the fiscal limits of the welfare state; it would tidy up the jumble of existing social market provisions in one neat package of cash grants; it would allow people to purchase their own provisions, thus shifting the focal point for distribution of welfare goods and services from the social to the economic market: and it would concentrate social provisions on those most in need.

Despite the apparent benefits of consolidating the broad spectrum of publicly financed social programs into one package of cash grants, there are several factors that militate against moving much further in this direction. The full impact of converting social welfare expenditures to cash grants large enough to eliminate poverty is difficult to predict. However, the disincentives to work and marital instability that surfaced in the Seattle and Denver Income Maintenance Experiments (see chaps. 2 and 5) do not reflect favorably on the prospects of this approach.[3] Moreover, direct cash grants are not a quick fix for many social problems. There are various groups of social welfare recipients such as the mentally retarded, delinquents, neglected children, alcoholics, teenage mothers, drug abusers and other social offenders, and the disoriented elderly, for whom provisions in the form of publicly sponsored services would be often more appropriate than direct cash grants. Thus, many programs would continue to operate in the social market even under an expanded system of cash grants.

Finally it would be difficult to muster broad public support for giving people who do not work as much money as those employed full time earning the minimum wage. Although the array of cash and in-kind benefits available to the poor might add up to the minimum wage, spread out in various programs it offers neither the convenience nor the clarity of a direct cash distribution. In some ways, inconvenience and obscurity are functional characteristics for the distribution of welfare provisions in a capitalist society. The inconvenience of having to make multiple applications and receiving vouchers and in-kind provisions instead of money injects a strain of the Protestant ethic into the dispensation of social benefits to people who may be employable. They too must "work" at obtaining support. And obscuring the total cash value of benefits available to the poor in a maze of social welfare programs avoids a direct confrontation with the disincentives to work that would threaten to undermine the unified cash grant approach.

Another way of looking at the trend in government spending for social welfare is to shift the comparative focus from the microlevel of individual citizens to the macrolevel of gross national product (GNP). Between 1940 and 1960 public expenditures for social welfare remained on an even keel, moving slightly from 9.2 to 10.0% of the gross national product. Over the next fifteen years, however, these expenditures rose rapidly from the 1960 level of 10.5 to 20% of the gross national product in 1975. As shown in Table 7.2, every category of social welfare expenditure increased significantly during this period; the field was led by social insurance and public aid, each with spending that multiplied more than tenfold. A more detailed breakdown of these categories (Table 7.3) reveals that this increase involved not only the growth of established benefits but also the addition of several large programs such as Medicare, food stamps, the

Economic Opportunity Program, and the Comprehensive Employment and Training Act initiated in the mid-1960s, which accounted for more than 10% of 1979 expenditures.

If the growth rate between 1960 and 1975 continued, the entire GNP would be consumed by public expenditures for social welfare within two generations—an imbalance between investment in productive and nonproductive activities by any definition. But such an extrapolation is notoriously misleading. It is submitted merely to underscore the dramatic rate of expansion that occurred during this period. Rarely do fiscal trends of this sort continue to accelerate at such an unusual pace. Indeed, in 1977 the growth rate had slowed down to the point that there was a slight decline in social welfare expenditures as a percentage of the GNP for the first time in more than two decades. By 1979 social welfare expenditures had slid back to 18.5% of the GNP from the 20.4% peak of 1976.

It is unclear whether the proportional reduction in social welfare expenditures signals a temporary lull in the expansion of the welfare state after a long period of high growth or reflects a more fundamental leveling in the pattern of development. There is no established fiscal ceiling on modern welfare states. Looking elsewhere in the world we find many industrial societies that spend more than 18 to 20% of their gross national product on social welfare.[4] Britain, for example, spent 28.8% of its gross national product on social welfare in 1975.[5] However, between 1960 and 1975 the rate of growth in social welfare expenditures relative to gross national product in Britain was a little less than two-thirds that of the United States.

The rapid fiscal growth of the American welfare state was accompanied by a change in the balance among local, state, and federal expenditures. Between 1960 and 1978 the federal share of public spending for social welfare rose from 47.7 to 60.9%. That increase was more than four times as large as the increase from 1950 to 1960.[6] The heightened centralization of social welfare financing under federal auspices was an important modification in the fiscal structure of the welfare state. But this change was a cumulative result of unregulated growth rather than a planned objective of public policy.

Two critical perspectives on the growth of social welfare expenditures help to explain the political opposition to the American welfare state that has emerged in the early 1980s. One view suggests that the

Table 7.2. Gross National Product and Social Welfare Expenditures under Public Programs, Selected Fiscal Years 1929–79
(In millions, except for percentages)

Item	1929	1940	1950	1955	1960	1965	1970	1975	1977	1978	1979
Gross national product*	$101,300	$95,400	$264,800	$381,000	$498,300	$658,000	$960,200	$1,452,300	$1,836,500	$2,043,400	$2,313,400
Total social welfare expenditures†	$3,921	$8,795	$23,508	$32,640	$52,293	$77,175	$145,856	$290,047	$360,925	$394,382	$428,333
Percent of gross national product	3.9	9.2	8.9	8.6	10.5	11.7	15.2	20.0	19.6	19.3	18.5
Social insurance	$342	$1,272	$4,947	$9,835	$19,307	$28,123	$54,691	$123,013	$160,883	$174,935	$193,588
Percent of gross national product	.3	1.3	1.9	2.6	3.9	4.3	5.7	8.5	8.8	8.6	8.4
Public aid	$60	$3,597	$2,496	$3,003	$4,101	$6,283	$16,488	$41,326	$53,266	$59,394	$64,649
Percent of gross national product	.1	3.8	.9	.8	.8	1.0	1.7	2.8	2.9	2.9	2.8
Health and medical programs	$351	$616	$2,064	$3,103	$4,464	$6,246	$9,907	$17,708	$20,409	$22,930	$24,496
Percent of gross national product	.3	.6	.8	.8	.9	.9	1.0	1.2	1.1	1.1	1.1
Veterans' programs	$658	$629	$6,866	$4,834	$5,479	$6,031	$9,078	$17,019	$19,015	$19,744	$20,455
Percent of gross national product	.6	.7	2.6	1.3	1.1	.9	.9	1.2	1.0	1.0	.9

Education	$2,434	$2,561	$6,674	$11,157	$17,626	$28,108	$50,845	$80,863	$93,921	$101,592	$108,279
Percent of gross national product	2.4	2.7	2.5	2.9	3.5	4.3	5.3	5.6	5.1	5.0	4.7
Other social welfare	$76	$116	$448	$619	$1,139	$2,066	$4,145	$6,947	$9,071	$10,563	$10,640
Percent of gross national product	.1	.1	.2	.2	.2	.3	.4	.5	.5	.5	.4
All health and medical care‡	$477	$782	$3,065	$4,421	$6,395	$9,535	$25,391	$51,673	$67,704	$76,928	$86,240
Percent of gross national product	.5	.8	1.2	1.2	1.3	1.4	2.6	3.6	3.7	3.8	3.7

Note: Through 1976, fiscal year ended June 30 for federal government, most states, and some localities; for federal government beginning 1977, fiscal year ended Sept. 30 (data for transition period July–Sept. 1976 not included).

*Before Jan. 1, 1960, for conterminous U.S.; beginning Jan. 1, 1960, includes Alaska and Hawaii.

†For the 50 states and the District of Columbia (and possessions where applicable); includes some expenditure abroad. Represents program and administrative expenditures from federal, state, and local public revenues (general and special), trust funds, and other expenditures under public law,

including workers' compensation and temporary disability insurance payments made through private carriers and self-insurers; includes construction costs of schools, hospitals, and other facilities and expenditures for housing (not shown separately). See Table 7.3 for components of categories.

‡Combines "health and medical programs" (above) with medical services provided in connection with social insurance, public aid, veterans' vocational rehabilitation, and antipoverty programs.

Source: Social Security Bulletin, Annual Statistical Supplement, 1980 (Washington, D.C.: U.S. GPO, 1981), p. 55.

Table 7.3. Social Welfare Expenditures under Public Programs, Fiscal Years 1929-79 (In millions)

Program	1929	1940	1950	1955	1960	1965	1970	1975	1978	1979
Total	$3,921.2	$8,795.1	$23,508.4	$32,639.9	$52,293.3	$77,175.3	$145,855.7	$290,047.3	$394,382.5	$428,332.9
Social insurance	342.2	1,271.8	4,946.6	9,834.9	19,306.7	28,122.8	54,691.2	123,013.1	174,934.8	193,587.8
OASDHI	—	40.4	784.1	4,436.3	11,032.3	16,997.5	36,835.4	78,429.9	117,431.9	131,750.6
Health insurance (Medicare)	—	—	—	—	—	—	7,149.2	14,781.4	25,189.2	29,154.8
Railroad retirement	—	116.8	306.4	556.0	934.7	1,128.1	1,609.9	3,085.1	4,019.8	4,310.6
Public employee retirement	113.1	283.4	817.9	1,388.5	2,569.9	4,528.5	8,658.7	20,118.6	29,935.8	33,773.9
Unemployment insurance and employment service	—	553.0	2,190.1	2,080.6	2,829.6	3,002.6	3,819.5	13,835.9	12,598.4	11,313.4
Railroad unemployment insurance	—	18.9	119.6	158.7	215.2	76.7	38.5	41.6	134.0	86.9
Railroad temporary disability insurance	—	—	31.1	54.2	68.5	46.5	61.1	32.9	73.4	65.6
State temporary disability insurance	—	—	72.1	217.5	347.9	483.5	717.7	990.0	1,124.6	1,177.6
Workers' compensation	229.3	259.2	625.1	943.0	1,308.5	1,859.4	2,950.4	6,479.1	9,616.9	11,109.2
Public aid	60.0	3,597.0	2,496.2	3,003.0	4,101.1	6,283.4	16,487.8	41,326.4	59,394.3	64,648.8
Public assistance	59.9	1,124.3	2,490.2	2,941.1	4,041.7	5,874.9	14,433.5	27,378.5	37,208.3	40,702.3
Supplemental security income	—	—	—	—	—	—	—	6,091.6	7,193.7	7,532.3
Food stamps	—	—	—	—	—	35.6	577.0	4,693.9	5,139.5	6,478.1
Other*	.1	2,472.7	6.0	61.9	59.4	373.0	1,477.3	3,162.4	9,852.8	9,936.1
Health and medical programs	351.1	615.5	2,063.5	3,103.1	4,463.8	6,246.4	9,906.8	17,707.5	22,930.1	24,496.2
Hospital and medical care	146.3	343.0	1,222.3	2,042.4	2,853.3	3,452.3	5,313.4	9,407.0	10,670.3	11,628.0
Maternal and child health program	6.2	13.8	29.8	92.9	141.3	227.3	431.4	545.5	663.5	689.5
Medical research	—	2.6	69.2	132.8	448.9	1,165.2	1,635.4	2,646.0	3,981.0	4,225.0
School health (education agencies)	9.4	16.4	30.6	65.9	101.0	142.2	246.6	321.0	394.0	410.0
Other public health activities	88.8	154.5	350.8	383.7	401.2	671.0	1,348.0	2,919.0	5,043.0	5,877.0
Medical-facilities construction	100.4	85.2	360.8	385.4	518.1	588.3	932.1	1,869.0	2,178.3	1,666.7

Veterans' program	657.9	629.0	6,865.7	4,833.5	5,479.2	6,031.0	9,078.0	17,018.8	19,744.1	20,455.3
Pensions and compensation	434.7	443.3	2,092.1	2,689.7	3,402.7	4,141.4	5,398.8	7,578.5	9,676.5	10,556.9
Health and medical programs	50.9	75.8	748.0	761.1	954.0	1,228.7	1,784.0	3,516.8	5,237.5	5,552.5
Education	—	—	2,691.6	706.1	409.6	40.9	1,018.5	4,433.8	3,405.6	2,813.4
Life insurance	136.4	77.0	475.7	490.2	494.1	434.3	502.3	556.0	614.3	638.2
Welfare and other	35.8	32.9	858.3	186.5	218.8	185.8	379.4	933.7	810.2	892.3
Education	2,433.7	2,561.2	6,674.1	11,157.2	17,626.2	28,107.9	50,845.5	80,863.2	101,591.6	108,278.8
Housing	4.2	4.2	14.6	89.3	176.8	318.1	701.2	3,171.7	5,224.7	6,225.8
Other social welfare	76.2	116.4	447.7	619.0	1,139.4	2,065.7	4,145.2	6,946.6	10,562.9	10,640.2
Vocational rehabilitation	1.6	4.2	30.0	42.4	96.3	210.5	703.8	1,036.4	1,297.6	1,309.2
Institutional care	74.7	62.4	145.5	195.3	420.5	789.5	201.7	296.1	410.1	444.0
Child nutrition programs	—	4.0	160.2	239.6	398.7	617.4	896.0	2,517.6	3,585.0	3,988.6
Child welfare	—	45.0	104.9	135.1	211.5	354.3	585.3	597.0	800.0	800.0
Special OEO and ACTION program	—	—	—	—	—	51.7	752.8	638.3	881.4	896.9
Social welfare, not elsewhere classified†	—	.9	7.1	6.5	12.4	42.3	1,005.6	1,861.2	3,588.8	3,251.5

Note: Expenditures from federal, state, and local revenues (general and special) and trust funds and other expenditures under public law; includes capital outlays and administrative expenditures, unless otherwise noted. Includes some payments abroad. Through 1976, fiscal year ended June 30 for federal government, most states, and some localities; for federal government beginning 1977, fiscal year ended Sept. 30 (data for transition period July 1–Sept. 1976 not included).

*Work relief, other emergency aid, surplus food for the needy repatriate and refugee assistance, and work-experience training programs under the Economic Opportunity Act and the Comprehensive Employment and Training Act.

†Federal expenditures include administrative and related expenses of the Secretary of Health, Education, and Welfare and of the Social and Rehabilitation Service; Indian welfare and guidance; aging, and juvenile delinquency, and certain manpower and human development activities. State and local expenditures include amounts for antipoverty and manpower programs, day care, child placement and adoption services, foster care, legal assistance, care of transients, and other unspecified welfare services; before 1969–70, these amounts were included with institutional care.

Source: Social Security Bulletin, Annual Statistical Supplement, 1980 (Washington, D.C.: U.S. GPO, 1981), p. 56.

structural properties of a capitalist society place a stern limit on the extent to which income can be taxed for public expenditures on social welfare; it is held that beyond this unspecified, but meager, limit, the growth of social welfare retards capital accumulation and diverts income away from investments in productive economic activities. This view is taken from both ends of the political spectrum. On the right it is used to support charges that the expansion of the welfare state has contributed to the economic recession of the 1980s. On the left it is used to demonstrate that capitalist society is incompatible with anything more than a token welfare state. From this "structuralist" perspective, the growth of social welfare is seen as creating a systemic crisis, the remedy of which calls for taking extreme measures against either the welfare state or the capitalist system.[7]

In contrast to the structuralist view, Hirschman offers an interesting alternative explanation for the adversities experienced by the American welfare state as it entered the 1980s. This explanation suggests that the problems of the welfare state derive not so much from its size, which is modest in comparison to those in many other industrial societies, as from its precipitant rate of growth since 1960. As previously noted, social welfare expenditures as a proportion of the gross national product doubled between 1960 and 1976. Hirschman observes that such a rapid expansion of the supply of goods and services "is likely to bring with it a *deterioration in their quality* in relation to expectations, and that this quality decline produces disaffection with the performance of the public sector. If this argument has merit the problem is not all that fundamental, for the quality decline may well be temporary."[8] From this perspective the difficulties of the welfare state are interpreted more as growing pains than as symptoms of having exceeded a critical limit of expenditure.

The fiscal limits of the welfare state are ultimately a matter of political compromise informed by prevailing social values and tempered by the availability of economic surplus. Between 1960 and the late 1970s significant changes in the fiscal dimensions of the American welfare state occurred in the virtual absence of deliberate political debate on the rate or limits of growth. To the extent that the expansion of the welfare state was mediated by political considerations, they were concerned primarily with judging the legitimacy of claims to social provisions by numerous client groups. These judgments followed the distributive impulses of what Lowi terms "interest group liberalism."[9] As the needs of the poor, the elderly, the disabled, single parents, ethnic minorities, children, women, and various other groups were documented and brought before legislators, new programs were initiated and old ones extended. Little thought was given to the welfare state's capacity to manage such an accelerated rate of growth. Often, program implementation lagged well behind schedule, and agencies were unable to spend all the funds appropriated for new social initiatives.[10] With the narrow focus of concern on each claimant group's entitlements to social provisions, pluralism prevailed while a larger vision of an appropriate balance between the social and economic markets of welfare capitalism went wanting.

While a good deal of the growth in welfare expenditures was stimulated by interest groups claiming their due, these groups were often encouraged by planners and public officials well disposed toward expanding the functions and objectives of social welfare.[11] Public expenditures on social welfare are, in part, responsive to wishes and beliefs about the degree of good that might be accomplished through the social market. In the 1960s and 1970s the wishes and beliefs of social welfare advocates raised expectations about the range of social problems the welfare state could prevent and the extent to which it could improve the general quality of life. Despite almost two decades of expansion, these high expectations were disappointed. The political opposition that had coalesced by 1980 is in some degree a response to the failures to achieve the enlarged objectives of social welfare.

In probing the limits of the welfare state we are drawn to the questions of its proper functions and objectives. How far can the functions of social welfare extend before they intrude on the heartland of the market economy? To what extent can the objectives of social welfare go beyond protection from economic deprivation and provision of social care for those in need to the prevention of troubles and the promotion of happiness?

PREVENTING TROUBLES AND PROMOTING HAPPINESS

In the mid-1970s primary prevention was heralded as an idea whose time had come for firm endorsement by the social market.[12] This arrival was fueled to no small degree by federal funds from the National Institute of Mental Health, which supported professional training programs for primary prevention. Federal funding aside, the appeal of this idea is easy to understand; it holds out the implicit promise of reducing poverty, delinquency, mental illness, drug addiction, child abuse, and other seemingly intractable problems. Yet for all its appeal, there is a discomforting vagueness, a huge zone of uncertainty between the implicit promise and the application of primary prevention in the social market. Before exploring this zone of uncertainty, we should survey the semantics of preventive methods.

The term *primary prevention* is drawn from the nomenclature of public health: it is *primary* only in contrast to *secondary* and *tertiary* prevention. To prevent means to keep from happening, and that is what primary prevention is about. The social problem, be it mental retardation, drug abuse, poverty, suicide, or some other affliction, is averted either by doing something to the at-risk population that strengthens their immunity and resistance or by doing something to diminish the social conditions that breed the problem. Secondary prevention involves early diagnosis and treatment of the problem. The objective is to minimize the impact and duration of the problem, curing it as quickly as possible. Tertiary prevention involves therapeutic activities aimed to keep the problem from getting worse and to rehabilitate the client. The use of the terms *secondary* and *tertiary prevention* to describe efforts at cure and relief merely extends the old-fashioned objective of treatment, a creditable activity in its own right.

Conceptual nuances aside, there is an important practical distinction between the primary level and the secondary/tertiary levels of prevention. This involves the dimension of time. Primary prevention takes place *before* the problem has struck or at least at some incipient stage at which its symptoms are barely discernible.[13]

Because of its advanced timing, primary prevention of social problems could eliminate a great deal of human suffering. But there are three fundamental constraints that limit the scope of preventive activity in the social market. These constraints involve (1) the identification of client groups, (2) the unanticipated consequences of intervention, and (3) the social market's capacity for implementation of preventive schemes.

The advanced timing of primary prevention creates a formidable issue of client identification in regard to social problems. If the problem is not evident at the moment, how does one know the particular group of people in need of primary prevention? The issue is less tangled in secondary and tertiary prevention. When the problem—drug abuse, child abuse, unemployment—is present, there is pain, and clients either identify themselves and come forward for help or they are referred by family, friends, clergy, the courts, and other community agencies. When the problem is not immediately felt by the client it falls to policy analysts and social welfare planners to define *populations at risk*, which become the target groups for preventive efforts. It is here that the issue of client identification becomes a most delicate matter.

To illustrate the issue, let us imagine a conference of social welfare planners (perhaps on primary prevention) in which one of the participants comes down with a contagious disease. Upon discovery of this dangerous situation public health officials declare all the participants to be a "high risk" group that is to receive the proper inoculation immediately. Most of the participants at the conference would probably feel some anxiety at the same time that they would be thankful for the remarkable safeguards of primary prevention that are available. But what would happen and how would they feel if the "at risk" label related to a social problem rather than a contagious disease? How would they respond if their children were to be designated as "at risk" of becoming delinquents based on assessments from a predelinquent screening program of the type proposed in the early 1970s by one of President Nixon's advisers? Or if they were members of an ethnic group that was identified as "at risk" of having out-of-wedlock births—and found their neighborhoods being canvassed by planned parenthood workers? Or if they were divorced or separated parents and discovered that their children have been identified by the National Institute of Mental Health Office of Prevention as a special "high risk" population in regard to mental health problems?[14]

It is unlikely that these types of judgments (however firm the data bases from which they are drawn) and the accompanying labels would be borne with the same degree of equanimity as in the previous example of exposure to a contagious disease. The latter was basically an impersonal event that carried no stigma or connotation of individual responsibility. In contrast, many social problems attach both stigma and, in the public eye, some degree of individual responsibility to people who are experiencing the problems or who are somehow judged to be at risk of getting them. There is often a wide margin of error in predicting those at risk. Moreover, there is not always normative agreement about what constitutes a social problem. Various groups consider high rates of divorce and some types of drug use as indicative of new freedoms instead of social problems. And planned parenthood programs sometimes have been accused of promoting racial genocide rather than preventive practice.[15]

The crux of this issue is how the targets of primary prevention can be identified without doing harm to the target group in the process by creating stigma, a negative self-image, or just plain psychological discomfort among the designated "at-risk" population. The "self-fulfilling prophecy" of labeling is a well-known phenomenon in social science.[16] The dilemma in preventive efforts is that the label *at-risk* may precipitate or contribute to the problem it predicts.

The more universal the criteria that distinguish populations at risk, the less likely these groups are to experience stigma and other negative effects of the identification. Thus, it has been proposed that preventive policies be designed around universal criteria which define at-risk populations not in relation to specific social problems (that is, delinquency, illegitimacy, child abuse, unemployment) but rather to normal periods of stress and vulnerability that may trigger problems and to which the vast majority of society is exposed (for example, pre- and postnatal periods, loss of income, death in the family, and retirement).[17] While the identification of target populations according to these developmental and situational crises mitigates the problems of stigmatization, it leaves the process of identifying specific clients in a haze of abstraction. There is an unspecified number of stress-producing life changes beginning with birth followed by entering school, adolescence, school graduation, marriage, parenthood, divorce, finding a job, losing a job, moving, death in the family, career promotions, severe illness, retirement, and aging to mention the most obvious. Some of these events are experienced more than once. It appears that most people's natural coping skills are adequate to deal successfully with many of these stressful experiences (some people even pride themselves on being able to muster the personal resources to cope with life's hardships).

The difficulty here is that of translating general guidelines for preventive policy into specific applications. It would be very expensive to deliver widespread preventive services to all the groups experiencing stressful life changes. And if such widespread preventive services were available it is unclear how they might affect the natural coping skills that individuals possess. (Is it possible that over time these skills may atrophy?) Moreover, in using universal criteria such as stressful life changes to identify populations at risk, one cannot ignore the *degree* of risk. If only a minority of those experiencing these stressful events are unable to cope with them successfully, at what point are policymakers better advised to offer treatment to the relatively few who experience problems than to try to prevent the difficulty for the many (most of whom can handle the stress on their own and might even be the better for it)?

The second limiting condition pertains to the knowledge base of primary prevention. Knowledge about how to prevent problems is tenuous at best. Proposals for primary prevention efforts are based frequently on plausible theory or popular ideas which may produce results that are contrary to their good intentions. For example, the sharp increase in out-of-wedlock births among teenagers in recent years (from 16 per 1,000 in 1960 to 25 per 1,000 in 1975) is a growing national problem. Among the common proposals for primary prevention in this area are (a) providing adolescents easy access to free family planning services without the requirement of parental consent, (b) offering specially designed sex education programs for adolescents in public schools, and (c) the provision of free or low-cost abortion services.[18] Whether or not one would support these measures on moral or religious grounds, they represent on face value a logical preventive approach to the problem at hand. If these preventive measures were widely instituted it is possible that the proportion of out-of-wedlock births among sexually active teenagers would decrease to some degree. At the same time, however, it is also possible that the sanction of sexually active behavior by the schools, hospitals, government, and community agencies which is implicit in these measures might induce some portion of the 50% of youths under 18 who, research indicates, are not presently sexually active to give it a try.[19] Thus, the overall consequences of these measures might produce a decrease in the *proportion* of out-of-wedlock births among sexually active teenagers and an increase in the absolute number of these births (because more teenagers are sexually active).[20]

Finally, if questions of client identification can be resolved and preventive measures can be proved to work without negative side effects, judicious thought must be given to the social market's capacity for implementation. Successful demonstrations of primary prevention programs usually involve services carefully provided to a circumscribed population by a well-trained staff of highly motivated professionals. A classic case is the Headstart program, which was launched under the Economic Opportunity Act in the summer of 1965. The idea for this effort drew heavily on the experimental studies of Martin Deutsch and his colleagues, who worked closely with a group of preschool children from disadvantaged backgrounds. Deutsch's painstaking efforts, which included a variety of techniques to stimulate intellectual and emotional development, produced a relatively successful demonstration of how early high-level professional intervention with a small group under carefully controlled circumstances could strengthen intellectual and social development of children from disadvantaged backgrounds.[21] However, the staff, commitment, and working conditions at the New York Medical College where Deutsch experimented could hardly be replicated in thousands of public schools across the country. The Headstart program emerged as the shadow of Deutsch's work, and national results were considerably less substantial than the original project.[22]

In the Milwaukee Project intense work with infants of retarded mothers produced a significant increase in the children's IQs by the time they reached school age.[23] Whether professional standards and levels of effort could be maintained if the technology of this type of experimental project were transferred to a national program is the sort of question to which advocates of primary prevention in the social market must attend more carefully than in the past.

There is a lesson to be remembered from the early 1960s, when welfare state planners convinced Congress that social services could prevent economic dependency. The 1962 service amendments to the Social Security Act were based on the premise that increased resources for the provision of intensive social casework services for recipients and potential recipients of public assistance would effectively reduce the public assistance rolls. The notion was supported by preliminary reports of success from demonstration projects which were accepted with insufficient caution and discrimination.[24] However, casework's preventive and curative powers never had a real test because the supply of qualified workers was severely inadequate for the task. To implement the 1962 service amendments an estimated 31,000 professional social workers were needed by 1970. By 1965 public welfare agencies employed fewer than 2,500 professional social workers and fewer than 3,000 professionals were being trained annually for all public and private programs.[25] The truly disturbing factor, according to Steiner, "is that it was always obvious that personnel to do the job were not available."[26] When the public assistance rolls increased by almost 1 million recipients between 1962 and 1966 instead of shrinking, social casework services suffered an immense loss of credibility.[27] The unfortunate consequence of this experience was that potentially positive outcomes of these services—which may be more modest than the prevention of dependency but nonetheless humane and useful—were lost. Such is the penalty for misjudging the capacities of the social market in the realm of preventive action.

Just as the prevention of troubles is often beyond the power and scope of the social market, so too is the promotion of happiness. Of all the political ideals, Karl Popper reminds us, "that of making people happy is perhaps the most dangerous one. It leads invariably to the attempt to impose our scale of 'higher' values upon others, in order to make them realize what seems to us of greatest importance for their happiness; in order, as it were, to save their souls."[28] In a similar vein, to design social welfare provisions that will improve the general quality of life requires first making value judgments as to what constitutes a "higher quality" of living. Universal agreement is difficult to achieve on questions of this sort. Popper suggests, as a guiding principle of social reform, that fighting against the greatest, most urgent evils of society is preferable to fighting for its greatest ultimate good.[29] According to this principle the social market is better suited to the protection from want than the promotion of happiness.

Emphasizing this protective character of the social market, Sidney Webb was among the first proponents of the modern welfare state to endorse the idea of a national minimum. As Webb saw it, entitlement to a minimum standard of welfare would not interfere with the efforts of individuals to better their socioeconomic circumstances and rise above the mean. He observed that "the illimitable realm of the upward" could be left open, while "by fencing off the downward way, we divert the forces of competition along the upward way."[30] Commitment to a national minimum focuses welfare provisions upon those groups in the greatest social, economic, and physical distress. The concentration of benefits on these needy people permits the welfare state to perform a redistributive function in society.

The formulation of a just national minimum standard involves a continuous and an enormously complex process of political compromise. Yet the imposing political demands of that process are dwarfed by the elusive metaphysical requirements of promoting happiness. Whereas there is much room for variations in the magnitude of welfare provisions that plausible definitions of a minimum standard might encompass, there are virtually no bounds to the range of welfare provisions that might conceivably enhance the pursuit of happiness. Still, there is some point along a theoretical continuum between the reduction of suffering and the promotion of happiness at which, as minimal standards are elevated, tangible distinctions based on benefit levels grow faint. At that transition point the line dividing these two objectives dissolves into intentions and predispositions.

By the mid-1970s this line had been crossed as objectives of the welfare state moved beyond concerns for the reduction of economic dependency and deprivation to the mission of enhancing human development and the quality of life. As previously noted (in chap. 3), this movement advanced by degrees under the auspices of various public measures such as the Community Mental Health Centers Act of 1963, the Older Americans Act of 1965, and the 1967 and 1974 amendments to the Social Security Act. The movement received symbolic confirmation in the rechristening of what remained of the Department of Health, Education and Welfare (since Education achieved independent status) as Health and Human Services. The term *welfare* with its connotation of need and concerns for basic maintenance, appears to be out of favor.

TRANSFORMATION OF THE WELFARE STATE: 1960–80

But more than a name is at stake. Since 1960 the American welfare state has undergone significant changes in the absence of a coherent social philosophy to guide its development. These changes have reshaped several basic dimensions of the social market along the following lines.

Size

There has been substantial growth in public expenditures for social welfare from $52.3 billion in 1960 to $428.3 billion in 1979. As already shown, these figures represent an increase from 10.5 to 18.5% of the gross national product. That increase is particularly notable in light of the relatively steady state of social welfare expenditures from 1940 to 1960, during which time they varied between 9 and 10% of the GNP. Measured by its consumption of societal resources, the size of the social market has almost doubled in less than two decades.

Auspices

The growth of the welfare state has been accompanied by changes in responsibility for the financing and delivery of benefits. Public responsibility for financing social welfare has increased. From 1950 to 1965 the relationship between public and private expenditures for social welfare remained fairly constant, with public funds accounting for about 65% of all social welfare expenditures. By 1978 the public share had risen to over 70% of all social welfare expenditures. This development is part of a larger movement toward federal hegemony in the fiscal affairs of the welfare state. Between 1960 and 1978, as public contributions gained over private financing, within the public sector the federal share had expanded from less than half to over 60% of social welfare expenditures. While fiscal responsibility for the welfare state has become more centralized under federal auspices, responsibility for the delivery of benefits has become more dispersed. As discussed earlier (chap. 1) public financing has not only stimulated the delivery of social welfare benefits by numerous voluntary nonprofit agencies through purchase-of-service arrangements, it has opened participation in the social market to proprietary agencies as well.

Benefit Structure

Since 1960 the range of provisions in the social market has broadened to include a variety of benefits such as meals, food stamps, transportation, medical care, legal aid, community mental health, and day-care services (see chap. 3). This diversification of social provisions reflects a notable change in the overall benefit structure of the welfare state. As provisions have become more varied there has been a substantial increase in the proportion of benefits in-kind versus cash benefits allocated through the social market. One estimate indicates that the proportion of in-kind benefits more than doubled from 12 to 27% of all federal expenditures on human resources between 1961 and 1976.[31] Other data reveal that between 1965 and 1980 the value of in-kind benefits in the form of food, housing, and medical care surged from $2.2 billion to more than $72.5 billion (or $27.7 billion in constant 1965 dollars). Over that same period expenditures on the portion of these major in-kind benefits that went exclusively to the poor rose from one-half to twice the value of cash aid provided through means-tested public assistance.[32] Thus, by 1980 the social market was distributing $2 worth of in-kind benefits for each $1 of cash assistance allocated to the poor, a complete reversal in the balance of in-kind versus cash provisions under the 1965 benefit structure.

Clientele

Between 1960 and 1980 the composition of the welfare state clientele was altered as a growing number of nonpoor consumers, many of whom came from the middle class, qualified for benefits. This drift toward universalism was given impetus by the liberal design of eligibility requirements, which made services available to people well above the poverty level in many programs (examined in chap. 3). By the early 1970s the results of this trend were reflected in the declining portion of social welfare expenditures in the federal budget focused exclusively on the poor. From 1973 to 1976 federal expenditures on human resource programs that were not solely for the poor increased from 46.5 to 54% of the total budget outlay. At the same time, expenditures on programs earmarked for the poor declined from 11.2 to 9.4% of the total budget.[33] During this period of decline the official poverty count had climbed slightly from 11.1 to 11.8% of the population.

Purpose

Finally, the objectives of the welfare state have moved beyond the provision of social care and protection for those in need. As expressed in the expanding range of social welfare benefits and the changing composition of the clientele, between 1960 and 1980 a broader mission was fashioned to encompass the goals of enhancing human development and improving the quality of life. Commenting on this broader mission, Kristol observes that the welfare state "lost its original self-definition and became something more ambitious, more inflated, and incredibly more expensive. It became the paternalistic state, addressing itself to every variety of 'problem' and committed to 'solving' them all—committed, that is, to making human life unproblematic."[34]

These changing dimensions of the welfare state raise issues of vision and intent: As in-kind benefits proliferated, to what extent did social welfare policymakers consider the desirability of a reversal in the balance of in-kind provisions relative to the amount of cash benefits for the poor? To what extent do the substantial fiscal growth and changing composition of social welfare clientele represent the consequences of a purposeful design? Indeed, to what extent have any of these trends been informed by some larger sense of the future of the welfare state? As these questions suggest, one might imagine that changes of such scope and importance were carefully debated and ultimately guided by a deliberate vision of how the welfare state should develop. Instead, it appears that these trends reflect a collection of discrete programs that were designed with faint consideration for the larger changes to which they contributed. From the early 1960s to 1975 the number of federal domestic grant-in-aid programs rose from about 200 to more than 1,100.[35] Such a flurry of activity no doubt blurred perceptions of change in the overall structure of the welfare state.

The larger picture, of course, is always more vivid in retrospect. The problem, however, is not so much the myopic vision of social welfare planners as the apparent blindness to broad principles that lend form and substance to the welfare state. Questions about universalism versus selectivity, provisions in cash versus in-kind, profit versus nonprofit providers, and the rate and limits of fiscal growth of the welfare state are matters of basic principle. Between 1960 and 1980 these matters were decided almost unintentionally by accretion rather than by deliberation. Over that period the welfare state was transformed through a process of unbridled incrementalism, a process that had little regard for estimating the workable limits of the social market.

In his keynote speech at the American Public Welfare Association's fiftieth anniversary, Pulitzer Prize-winning author Edgar May remarks on the neglect to define limits of the welfare state and some of its consequences. He observes that "in five decades of developing this safety net we have failed to talk clearly about its limits. We have failed to illuminate the boundaries of income maintenance and social service programs. We have sometimes left the public confused, believing that the systems designed to relieve poverty should categorically eliminate it. When they don't we are left with greater frustration and skepticism."[36] Part of the frustration referred to by May stems from a quirk of human nature whereby the absence of limits tends to deprive us of a sense of success. When prospects are boundless, achievements are likely to fall short of expectations. There has been a "certain nonlinearity," as Moynihan puts it, "between the number of categorical aid programs issuing forth from Washington and the degree of social satisfaction that has ensued."[37]

By 1980 the deepening economic recession provoked vigorous political opposition to the welfare state against which the record of almost two decades of intemperate and disjointed growth offered little resistance. In place of the openhanded benevolence of interest-group liberalism, the tightfisted, calculating principles of the market economy have been invoked to regulate and shape the future of the welfare state in the 1980s. Although the burgeoning welfare state needs systematic adjustments and regulation, too great a reliance on capitalist doctrine to supply the methods of control will surely have a chilling effect on the communal spirit of compassion and responsibility which contributes to the essential nature of the welfare state. The issue is a matter of degree and proportion which calls for a balanced approach. Neither romantic nostalgia for the turbulent War on Poverty nor unconditional faith in the smooth invisible hand of the market economy is a prudent sentiment to guide the evolution of the welfare state. A fresh vision of welfare capitalism is required, one that contemplates the basic dimensions of the welfare state and the appropriate relationships between social and economic markets.

NOTES

1. The human investment model of development emphasizes the positive effects that social welfare measures may have upon production. As Rys explains, "To the extent that measures designed to insure against risk, provide medical care, and assure rehabil-

itation of the disabled concentrate on the physical aspects of preservation of human resources, they facilitate the development of economic activities and the improvement of rates of productivity" (Vladimir Rys, "Social Security and Social Planning in Contemporary Society," in *The Planning of Social Security* [Geneva: International Social Security Association, 1971] p. 65). Also see Everett M. Kassalow, ed., *The Role of Social Security in Economic Development* (Washington, D.C.: U.S. Dept. of Health, Education and Welfare, 1968).

2. Charles A. Murray, "The Two Wars Against Poverty: Economic Growth and the Great Society," *Public Interest*, 69 (Fall 1982), 8–10.

3. Michael Keeley et al., "The Labor-Supply Effects and Costs of Alternative Negative Income Tax Programs," *Journal of Human Resources*, 13 (Winter 1978), 3–26; Michael Hannan, Nancy Brandon Tuma, and Lyle Groeneveld, "Income and Marital Events: Evidence From an Income Maintenance Experiment," *American Journal of Sociology*, 82 (May 1977), 1186–211.

4. In 1966, for example, there were at least 10 nations with social security expenditures twice as large as that of the United States relative to their gross national products. For comparative expenditure figures see Harold Wilensky, *The Welfare State and Equality* (Berkeley: University of California Press, 1975), pp. 122–23, and Alfred Kahn and Sheila Kammerman, *Social Services in International Perspective* (Washington, D.C.: U.S. GPO, 1977).

5. Ian Gough, *The Political Economy of the Welfare State* (London: Macmillan, 1979), p. 77.

6. Alma McMillan and Ann Kallman Bixby, "Social Welfare Expenditures, Fiscal Year 1978," *Social Security Bulletin*, 43 (May 1980), 11.

7. Albert Hirschman, "The Welfare State in Trouble," *American Economic Review*, 70 (May 1980), 113–16.

8. Ibid., p. 114.

9. Theodore Lowi, *The End of Liberalism* (New York: Norton, 1969).

10. In the Model Cities program, for example, only 15 of the 65 cities that had completed their first program year managed to spend more than 50% of their funded budgets, which they requested after at least one year of planning. For details, see Neil Gilbert and Harry Specht, *The Dynamics of Community Planning* (Cambridge, Mass.: Ballinger, 1977), p. 59. Since the 1970s there has been a growing body of literature addressed to the problems of program implementation. The seminal works in this area include Jeffrey L. Pressman and Aaron Wildavsky, *Implementation* (Berkeley: University of California Press, 1973), and Eugene Bardach, *The Implementation Game: What Happens After a Bill Becomes a Law?* (Cambridge, Mass.: MIT Press, 1977).

11. Martha Derthick offers a lucid illustration of how state planners were encouraged to exploit certain loopholes in the 1967 amendments to the Social Security Act by federal officials who expressed a "you hatch it, we match it" attitude toward growth of federally supported social services (*Uncontrollable Spending for Social Services Grants* [Washington, D.C.: Brookings Institution, 1975], pp. 7–14).

12. Donald Klein and Stephen Goldston, *Primary Prevention: An Idea Whose Time Has Come* (Rockville, Md.: National Institute of Mental Health, 1977).

13. It can be argued that treatment or secondary/tertiary prevention often crosses over into primary prevention in the sense that one problem, such as drug abuse, often generates another such as crime; thus, successful treatment of drug abuse may be said

to prevent crime. However, the *main objective* of secondary/tertiary prevention is to treat the existing problem, not to deal with its potential aftermath. It is only at the very high level of abstraction, where all problems and solutions can be seen as interrelated, that secondary and tertiary cross over into primary prevention. At that point the distinctions among primary, secondary, and tertiary lose all meaning.

14. Milton Wittman, "Preventive Social Work: What? How? Where?" paper presented at the Eleventh Annual Symposium on Issues in Social Work Education, Graduate School of Social Work, University of Utah, Apr. 17, 1980.

15. Neil Gilbert and Joseph Eaton, "Who Speaks for the Poor?" *Journal of the American Institute of Planners*, 36 (Nov. 1970), 415.

16. Robert K. Merton, *Social Theory and Social Structure* (New York: Free Press, 1957), pp. 421–36; Prudence Rains, "Imputations of Deviance: A Retrospective Essay on the Labeling Perspective," *Social Problems*, 23 (Oct. 1975), 1–11.

17. Gerald Caplan, *Support Systems and Community Mental Health* (New York: Behavioral Publications, 1974).

18. Catherine Chilman, "Teenage Pregnancy: A Research Review," *Social Work*, 24 (Nov. 1979), 492–98.

19. The 50% estimate is based on research cited in ibid.

20. Speculation of this sort has led to considering the possibility that drivers' education courses which qualify graduates for auto insurance deductions and generally encourage licensing of teenage drivers might lead to higher accident rates. While the evidence is not decisive, a study of 10 Connecticut towns that eliminated these courses showed a huge decrease in the number of 16- and 17-year-old drivers and a concurrent decline in the number of serious auto accidents. For studies in this area, see Leon S. Robertson and Paul L. Zader, "Driver Education and Fatal Crash Involvement of Teenaged Drivers," *American Journal of Public Health*, 68 (Oct. 1978), 959–65, and Leon S. Robertson, "Crash Involvement of Teenaged Drivers When Driver Education is Eliminated from High School," ibid., 70 (June 1980), 599–603.

21. Martin Deutsch, "Facilitating Development in the Preschool Child: Social and Psychological Perspectives," *Merrill-Palmer Quarterly*, 10 (1954), 249–63.

22. See, for example, the Westinghouse Learning Corporation evaluation, *The Impact of Head Start: An Evaluation of the Effects of Head Start on Children's Cognitive and Affective Development* (Athens: Ohio University Press, 1969).

23. F. Rick Heber, "Sociocultural Mental Retardation: a Longitudinal Study," in Donald Forgays, ed., *Primary Prevention of Psychopathology, Volume II, Environmental Influences* (Hanover, N.H.: University Press of New England, 1978), pp. 39–62.

24. Gilbert Steiner, *The State of Welfare* (Washington, D.C.: Brookings Institution, 1971), pp. 39–40.

25. Neil Gilbert and Harry Specht, *Dimensions of Social Welfare Policy* (Englewood Cliffs: Prentice-Hall, 1974), p. 100. In addition to the dearth of professional social workers available for jobs with departments of public welfare, those employed in these positions do not tend to stay very long. A study of turnover in New York City welfare agencies during 1964 reveals that 30% of the workers resigned within nine months of their appointment (Lawrence Podell, "Attrition of First-Line Social Service Staff," *Welfare in Review*, 5 [Jan. 1967], 9–14). In 1966 the national turnover rate for public

welfare agencies was 22.8%, almost double the turnover rate of all professionals in civil service positions on federal, state, and local levels at that time.

26. Steiner, *State of Welfare*, p. 39.

27. For further discussion see Neil Gilbert, "Transformation of Social Services," *Social Service Review*, 51 (Dec. 1977), 624–41; Elizabeth Wickenden, "A Perspective on Social Services: An Essay Review," *Social Service Review*, 50: 4 (Dec. 1976), 570–85; and Steiner, *State of Welfare*.

28. Karl Popper, *The Open Society and Its Enemies*, rev. ed. (Princeton: Princeton University Press, 1950), p. 422.

29. Ibid., p. 155.

30. Sidney Webb, *The Necessary Basis of Society*, 1908, pp. 11–12, quoted in William Robson, *Welfare State and Welfare Society* (London: Allen & Unwin, 1976), p. 21.

31. Henry J. Aaron, *Politics and the Professors: The Great Society in Perspective* (Washington, D.C.: Brookings Institution, 1978), p. 12. The calculation of in-kind benefits includes all noncash transfers for human resource programs.

32. Timothy Smeeding, *Alternative Methods for Valuing Selected In-Kind Transfer Benefits and Measuring Their Effects on Poverty*, U.S. Bureau of the Census, Technical Paper no. 50 (Washington, D.C.: U.S. GPO, 1982).

33. Aaron, *Politics and the Professors*, p. 13. Data from Smeeding, *Alternative Methods*, p. 3, reveal that from 1975 to 1980 in-kind transfers exclusively for the poor declined from 61 to 58% of in-kind benefits in the major areas of food, housing, and medical care.

34. Irving Kristol, *Two Cheers for Capitalism* (New York: Mentor, 1978), p. 231.

35. David Stockman, "The Social Pork Barrel," *Public Interest*, 39 (Spring 1975), 13.

36. Edgar May, "Fifty Years of Looking Ahead," *Public Welfare*, 38 (Fall 1980), 10.

37. Daniel P. Moynihan, "Toward a National Urban Policy," *Public Interest*, 17 (Fall 1969), 5.

EIGHT

THE MIDDLE COURSE: TOWARD SOCIAL RESPONSIBILITY IN A MIXED ECONOMY

Critical analyses of the American welfare state may be grouped broadly into two camps that hold opposing views on collective intervention and adhere to disparate visions of Utopia. Critics on the left perceive the welfare state as a cunning device that takes just enough of the edge off the hardships of capitalism to keep the masses in check without altering the basic inequities of the market economy.[1] While collective intervention is the elixir of the socialist Utopia to which this group is dedicated, they claim that the low dose of collectivism injected through the welfare state acts to preserve rather than transform the capitalist order. Critics on the right perceive the welfare state as an insidious agent slowly corroding the work ethic and the spirit of capitalism.[2] According to this view, collective intervention is undesirable in all but the most limited circumstances, which the welfare state has surpassed. Any further expansion of the welfare state is seen as a threat to the Utopian paradigm of a free market adhered to by this group.

Defense of the welfare state rests on the middle ground between these two camps, where it is seen as neither a handmaiden to capitalist exploitation nor a usurper of freedom in the market economy. Rather, from this position the welfare state is considered a counterforce to balance against the excesses and hazards of capitalism without inhibiting the free market's productive energies. In the nature of things it is a delicate balance easily tipped.

There is a certain forensic utility to the handmaiden-usurper-counterforce classification of views on the welfare state in that it identifies the broad lines of debate. At the same time, it obscures some important distinctions. Each camp contains diverse ideas about the proper degree of collective intervention for a healthy society. These schools of thought range along a bell-shaped curve of tolerance for the welfare state. Tolerance of the welfare state is low at both ends of this curve, rising toward minimal acceptance up to a peak of positive endorsement at the center. Among the many positions on this curve there are three pairs, as depicted in Figure 8.1, that span the full range and possess a degree of symmetry between perspectives of the right and the left on the welfare state and political philosophies.

MARXISM AND SOCIAL DARWINISM

The modern welfare state is held in disdain by both Marxists on the far left and social Darwinists on the far right. The reasons for opposition by these groups, of course, differ.

The Marxist perspective takes a broader and more comprehensive view of social welfare than that embodied in the statutory provisions of the welfare state. Marxists are committed to a "welfare society" in which all economic affairs are conducted through the social market for the common benefit. The ideal vision of that society requires production, distribution, and consumption to be organized in line with the familiar dictum: "From each according to his ability, to each according to his needs."[3] For Marxists, social intervention thus extends beyond the traditional borders of the welfare state to shape the

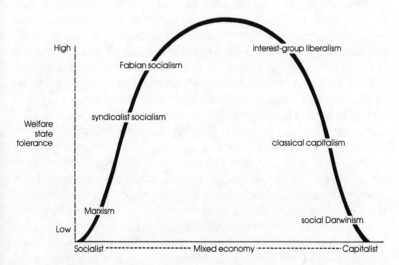

Figure 8.1.   Political Orientation and Tolerance of the Welfare State.

basic principles for production and distribution of material benefits throughout society.

Although the welfare state controls too small a proportion of material benefits to satisfy the Marxists' criteria for the good society, it could be seen as a foundation on which to build such a society.[4] In the main, however, that is not the view from the far left. At the core there are two reasons for the Marxists' aversion to the welfare state.

First is the view that piecemeal reforms of the welfare state cannot alter the basic capitalist mode of production or the structure of inequality to which it gives rise. Marxists claim that the ameliorative efforts of the welfare state ignore the root causes of inequality. Evidence for the continuing structure of inequality in the United States is often cited by social scientists using the percentage of aggregate income received by each fifth or tenth of the population.[5] These data indicate that the relative share of the bottom 20% of the American population has remained fairly stable, at about 5% of aggregate money income from 1955 to 1979, welfare state interventions notwithstanding.[6] One might infer along with Marxists and other critics of inequality that these figures represent the ossification of economic classes.

However, just as the definition of poverty is surrounded by controversy (noted in chap. 4), the measurement of inequality is also subject to dispute. Using percentages of aggregate income to establish trends in inequality ignores the degree to which income typically fluctuates with age. Generally, both the people who are just starting out in a career and the retired elderly receive less income than those in their mid-forties to mid-fifties. Among the 25% of households in 1974 that earned less than $5,000 annually, almost half were headed by persons over 65.[7] However, if we take into consideration that 71% of the elderly own their own homes and 54% have paid off their mortgages, this group's low income is to some extent offset by its possession of significant assets.[8] Indeed, it has been estimated that outright ownership of the average home provides an asset that places the owners in a position equivalent to the top 2 percent of wealth holders in the country.[9] The standard approach to measuring inequality is like a snapshot that freezes everyone at different phases in their life cycle in a single frame. This picture is insensitive to the impact of demographic changes such as the increasing proportion of elderly in the population. When life cycle earnings and demographic changes are taken into account in measuring income distribution a different picture emerges, one that reveals a 23% decline in inequality between 1947 and 1972.[10]

The Marxists' second brief against the welfare state is that its failure to achieve basic structural reform of the capitalist economy is compounded by its success in defusing social unrest. Some argue that the welfare state has achieved this result through the coercive social control of government bureaucracies. Others suggest that the masses have been pacified by the material inducements of state pensions and supplementary provisions. Whether welfare has, as Briggs puts it, "soothed the spirit, or perhaps, tamed it," is a moot point.[11] In either case it slaps a damp cloth on the embers of revolution which the Marxists are wont to fan.

In contrast to the Marxist view of the welfare state as a hindrance to the socialist revolution, social Darwinists consider it an obstacle to natural evolution. Both these schools of thought have a deterministic outlook on the progress of civilization. Marxists interpret laws of history based on economic relationships, which they see as impelling society toward "the negation of the negation": the revolutionary synthesis that would give rise to the socialist state.[12] Social Darwinists link the force of natural law to the idea that "tooth and claw" capitalism contributes to the perfection of man and the advancement of civilization. According to this Darwinian doctrine, competition in the market economy is the process through which the law of natural selection weeds out the least fit, leaving space and resources for the "fittest" to flourish. From this perspective any meddling with natural selection through government aid to the poor and other welfare state measures threatens the eventual bloom of humanity.

The Marxist and social Darwinist positions represent extreme points on the curve of welfare state tolerance. Modern versions of social Darwinism are occasionally expressed in public settings. And as Hofstadter observes, "the survival of the fittest" has acquired a permanent niche in the public mind. However, the influence of this school of thought on public affairs in American life ran its course in the early 1900s.[13] Although Marxist thought is still fashionable among some cadres of the left, its influence on the development of the American welfare state has been and remains negligible.

SYNDICALIST SOCIALISM AND CLASSICAL CAPITALISM

Syndicalist socialists rank somewhat higher in their support of collective intervention for social welfare than those of a laissez-faire-capitalist persuasion. Nevertheless, both schools of thought converge in their suspicion of the state and their antipathy toward the bureaucratic apparatus of central government. Although they are on opposite sides of the political spectrum, this affinity accounts for similarities in some of the policies each advocates.

While classical capitalists are no great champions of the welfare state, the degree to which they object to communal intervention is frequently exaggerated and confused with the position of social Darwinists. "Anarchy plus the constable," Carlyle's oft-quoted phrase, evokes a popular image of the classical capitalist society in which government's role is restricted to maintaining a modicum of law and order amid the rough and tumble of a competitive market economy. But this popular image is somewhat distorted. Even among the early founders of the classical school of economic thought, the proper role of government was never quite that limited. As Robbins points out, the writings of Adam Smith and Jeremy Bentham expressed a range of legitimate government functions that went well beyond those of the night watchman.[14] Among the modern standard bearers of the classical school both Friedman and Hayek recognize the need for government to provide at least minimal support for the poor and incompetent. Friedman allows for the legitimacy of "government action to alleviate poverty."[15] Indeed, he was one of the early proponents of a negative income tax scheme to reform financial assistance for the poor. In a similar vein, Hayek observes that "there can be no doubt that some minimum of food, shelter, and clothing sufficient to preserve health and the capacity to work, can be assured to everybody."[16]

Underlying this veneer of tolerance for the welfare state, however, are deeper concerns for individual freedom and commitments to the market economy.[17] Thus, for Friedman a virtue of the negative income tax proposal is that it would substitute a minimal level of cash support for the array of existing social welfare benefits, thereby dispensing with the vast welfare state bureaucracy that delivers these benefits.[18] According to his scheme, aid to the poor would be low enough to maintain an incentive to work, permit the expression of individual preferences in how the money is spent, and be administered in a manner that allows the least amount of government intervention in peoples' lives. Hayek also favors arrangements that would restrict the scope and power of central government and promote the expression of individual interests.[19]

There is, of course, little sympathy between the views of classical capitalism and syndicalist socialism on the legitimacy of private ownership in the market economy. Syndicalists prefer a society organized around the principle of industrial democracy, whereby workers have direct control over the means of production.[20] Wary of the potential for oppression under a centralized administration, syndicalist doctrine stresses the primacy of worker management and local authority over the centralist tendencies of state socialism. It is this resistance to the power of the state that unites classical capitalism with syndicalist socialism on important issues of public policy. Both schools of thought share a broad philosophical perspective on the virtues of decentralization, self-help, informal mediating structures such as family and voluntary organizations, and citizen participation in community affairs. Decentralization has, perhaps, the strongest endorsement and provides a unifying framework for this perspective.

Since 1960 the decentralist-participatory train of thought has gained momentum, exercising an increasing influence on the American welfare state. The mandates for "maximum feasible participation" under the Economic Opportunity Act of 1964 and for "widespread citizen participation" in the Demonstration Cities and Metropolitan Development Act of 1966 launched the citizen participation movement in social welfare planning at the local level. At the extreme, proponents of this movement sometimes pressed for community control of local institutions, an objective to which syndicalists certainly would take no exception. By 1975 much of the turmoil surrounding this movement subsided, signaling not the demise of citizen participation but its institutionalization.[21] In the early 1980s the climate of opinion under the Reagan administration has lent further impetus to policies promoting local voluntary efforts, informal support networks (noted in Chap. 6), and decentralization of federal control in the welfare state. At the same time, in Britain a revival of syndicalist sentiment among the left has stirred the call for a "more participative and decentralized form of service provision":[22] a form emphasizing the role of voluntary action, self-help, and community-based initiatives in the welfare state, which, incidently, dovetails rather well with the Thatcher administration's conservative orientation toward the welfare state.

FABIAN SOCIALISM AND INTEREST-GROUP LIBERALISM

Common to both these groups is their ameliorative approach to social problems. They support public intervention and expansion of the social market through the method of piecemeal reform. What is different are the philosophical ideals that motivate these reform efforts.

Fabius Maximus, the Roman general after whom the Fabians named their society, was known for his tactics of attrition, fighting small skirmishes, avoiding decisive battles. It is these tactics that mark the gradualist methods of Fabian socialism. The Fabians believe that the "permeation" of collectivist ideas and reforms will lead eventually to popular acceptance of socialist principles.[23] In the course of implementing these methods the Fabians were among the senior architects of the British welfare state.

In the mid-1950s, Richard Titmuss, one of the intellectual leaders of the Fabian movement, sought to enlarge their purview on the welfare state. He argued that the conceptual boundaries of the welfare state should be extended to include all collective interventions that might meet certain needs of the individual and serve the wider interests of society.[24] According to Titmuss, this full range of collective interventions includes three types of welfare benefits: social welfare benefits derived from social services, which form the conventional core of the welfare state; fiscal welfare benefits that are obtained through tax allowances and relief; and occupational welfare, which covers the various fringe benefits of employment.[25] Despite the theoretical appeal of this comprehensive vision of welfare, in practice the Fabians are more inclined to devise ameliorative reforms around the core elements of the welfare state than to press for broader structural change. They tolerate the mixed economy of welfare capitalism, patiently planning the dissolution of its capitalist elements. If asked about the future of the welfare state, a Fabian might reply that extending the social market step-by-step will result in the birth of a Utopian socialist society, though not, perhaps, in his lifetime.

Just as Fabian socialism provided the intellectual momentum for the British welfare state, interest-group liberalism was the dominant force in the growth of the American welfare state (noted in chap. 7) up through the late 1970s. Although interest-group liberalism is similarly committed to expanding the scope of governmental activities, there is no socialist beacon to guide its long view. The collectivist reforms endorsed by this liberal school of thought represent both the humanistic wish to improve social conditions and the pragmatic instinct to accommodate organized claims to public beneficence. These piecemeal reforms draw neither meaning nor inspiration from a Utopian vision of the good society.

Joining strong collectivist tendencies with a healthy regard for capitalism, the liberal creed advocates the development of a mixed economy. But it is a vague, almost negative prescription: not too much public, not too much private. At best this prescription connotes the "golden mean of moderation," at worst the "average endowment of mediocrity." The mixed economy lacks a clear sense of purpose and intimations of a desirable life that invigorate doctrines further to the right and left.

While supporting widespread collective intervention, liberal proponents of the American welfare state lack a coherent vision of the mixed economy that delineates the form and substance of the social market. As the capitalist component of the mixed economy threatens to eclipse the American welfare state in the 1980s, the liberal doctrine appears to be unable to illuminate the distinctive qualities of the social market.[26]

RATIONALIZATION OF THE MIXED ECONOMY: ISSUES FOR THE WELFARE STATE

Efforts to clarify the position of the welfare state in a mixed economy must address at least four central issues. These issues concern the purpose, domain, organization, and operation of the social market.

First and, perhaps, most profound is the question of purpose. Under a mixed economy the ship of state navigates a middle course between the Scylla and Charybdis of doctrinaire enticements. "The purpose of this voyage," as Pinker explains, "is not to discover new continents but to keep the ship afloat and steer clear of the various eldorados along the shore, where life is rumoured to be less arduous than life on board—rumours belied only by the warnings of fugitives from those alien shores, clamouring to be taken along."[27] "Staying afloat," is surely desirable, though not exactly an inspirational social purpose.

It is, perhaps, more encouraging to think of this journey along the middle course as a movement striving to achieve the proper balance between competing values that enhance the human condition. Liberty and security are among the most prominent of these values. If the balance is tipped too far in one direction liberty may be smothered in a thick blanket of collective security, too far in the other direction and collective security may be shattered by the unrestrained clash of individual interests. In the balance between freedom and security the social market lends its weight to security. The advancement of communal security, however, represents a narrow view of the social market's purpose in a mixed economy. A broader conception of purpose would further encompass the competing notions of equality: equality of material conditions and equality of opportunity, that mighty precipitator of material inequality. Here the social market leans toward reducing material inequality through the redistribution of resources.

In addition to concerns for security and equality, a comprehensive view of the purpose of the social market would include the functions of social integration and social control. From different analytic perspectives on the welfare state, the roles of social integration and social control are accorded varying degrees of emphasis in the overall scheme of purpose.[28] The coercive elements of social control, for example, are given prominent weight in Marxist assessments of the welfare state.[29] From a centrist perspective on the mixed economy security and equality are viewed as cardinal objectives of the social market. In order to hold the middle course, these objectives must be pursued with restraint. The critical issue in clarifying the purpose of the social market in a mixed economy is, thus, more a matter of degree than kind.[30] The purpose is not to achieve perfect equality of material conditions and total security but to create a social balance amid the play of opposing values. From this perspective the central puzzle is to determine the size of the safety net and the extent of redistribution through the social market that are necessary to sustain a dynamic equilibrium among the competing forces of a mixed economy.

Closely related to the question of purpose is the second issue, which concerns the domain of the social market. This issue may be examined on two levels, one more abstract than the other. At the higher level of abstraction the problem is to distinguish the extent to which the systems of fiscal and occupational welfare, identified by Titmuss, overlap with and should be considered part of the social market.[31] One reason for including occupational benefits within the domain of the social market is that most of them, such as health insurance premiums, are not taxed and others, such as pension contributions, are tax deferred until retirement and then subject to several tax advantages. Thus, even though workers and employers usually envision these benefits as a substitute for wages in their employment contract, the tax exempt status of the benefits causes them not to be officially recognized as income by the government. To the extent that these benefits escape being taxed, they may be construed as partially subsidized. The basis for this view, however, may be nullified by the Reagan administration's proposal to count the value of health insurance premiums as part of the employee's taxable income.[32] Overall, the case for including occupational benefits within the conceptual bounds of the social market is weak.[33] Whatever their tax treatment, these benefits are an integral part of the reward structure of the market economy. The distribution of occupational benefits is more responsive to individual initiative, ability, productivity, and the desire for profit than to need, dependency, and charitable impulses. They are motivated less by collective ambitions for security and equality than by entrepreneurial inducements, which vary from firm to firm. Thus, occupational benefits are well characterized, in Mishra's words, "as part of the 'social policy' of private enterprise."[34]

Fiscal welfare is more complex. Federally financed public housing, housing voucher schemes, and day-care services are generally perceived as social market allocations. The question is: To what extent are these directly subsidized provisions equivalent to fiscal measures such as tax deductions for interest payments on home mortgages and tax credits for the purchase of day-care services? Kristol argues that tax deductions are essentially incentives for encouraging personal expenditures toward socially desirable ends. To think of them as subsidies is, he notes, "implicitly asserting that all income covered by the general provisions of the tax laws belongs of right to the government, and what the government decides, by exemption or qualification, not to collect in taxes constitutes a subsidy."[35] In theory there is certainly a valid distinction between government encouraging individuals to spend their own money on certain provisions and government taking money from some people and giving it to others in the form of directly subsidized provisions. What complicates the issue is that in practice the objective consequences of both actions look quite similar. That is, individuals obtain goods and services for less than it would cost them through a purely economic transaction taking place in the absence of government intervention. To the extent that fiscal welfare measures are administered by the state and in some ways modify allocations of the market economy, they may be said to resemble instruments of the social market. However, the nature of fiscal welfare measures is such that they tend to provide the greatest benefit to people in the upper tax brackets, which does little to advance equality or security, the predominant functions of the social market.

At a more practical level we confront the following question: In a mixed economy, how much overlap between the social and economic markets is feasible in providing for such goods and services as housing, food, meals, clothing, child care, legal aid, recreation, education, health, counseling, transportation, and homemaker aid?

On this question, speaking of the British welfare state, Marshall claims that health, education, and personal social services (for example, counseling, child welfare, homemaker aid, and the like) and cash assistance are not only well suited for the social market but "the purest expression of its identity, clearly detached from the market economy."[36] Nevertheless he goes on to challenge the suitability of certain other welfare functions such as housing and school meals, which he thinks diminish the social market's identity. Marshall suggests that this type of in-kind support "seems to have been increasing in a haphazard manner and that changes are taking place which call for close examination with a view to finding some principles on which the division of functions between welfare and the market might be founded."[37] His statement is interesting from a comparative viewpoint. Within the overall increase in British social welfare expenditures, the relationship between proportions devoted to cash and in-kind benefits has remained fairly stable.[38] In contrast, the United States has experienced an extraordinary rise (noted in chap. 7) in the proportion of social welfare expenditures on in-kind benefits. If Marshall is disturbed by the haphazard expansion of social market functions in Britain, he no doubt would find the American experience even more disquieting.

Although a set of principles that delineates the correct range of social market activities would be most convenient, the few that exist are exceedingly restrictive. Friedman, for example, suggests that the proper scope of public intervention is limited to the areas that cannot be handled through the market economy. These areas include rule-maker and umpire functions, government actions in cases where voluntary exchange is costly and impractical, and intervention on paternalistic grounds.[39] According to these principles health, education, and most other social services would be excluded from the public domain of the social market. Marshall's reason for considering these functions within the purview of the social market rests mainly on the expression of "strong popular support" for such placement.[40] Popular support is, perhaps, necessary but hardly a sufficient principle for identifying the functional boundaries of the welfare state.

Whatever the range of functions that by principle or tradition fall within the boundaries of the welfare state, there are various ways to organize them. The third major issue in the design of the social market is that of distinguishing the types of activities that are best conducted through centralized organization from those most compatible with decentralized arrangements. There are technical as well as political facets to this issue.

The character of some technical considerations is colorfully illustrated in Moynihan's criticism of proposals for organizing certain public health measures in New York City. These proposals advise that a rat control program be centralized while poison control centers be made a local responsibility. Taking exception to those arrangements, Moynihan notes that "the urban rat is preeminently a neighborhood type, preferring when possible, never even to cross the street. As for rodent control, opinion is universal (as best I know) that the fundamental issue is how individual homonids maintain their immediate surroundings." The basic solution, he suggests, "comes down, alas, to the question of keeping lids on garbage cans," a matter handled most conveniently at the neighborhood level.[41] By contrast, poison control centers require a level of skill and resources unlikely to be found in city neighborhoods. These centers are primarily designed to provide doctors information about the chemical nature of possibly harmful substances ingested by persons either accidently or with intent to damage themselves. That type of function can be exceedingly well fulfilled through a centralized delivery system. As Moynihan observes, a good case can be made for a national center under which one telephone number anywhere in the country would put a doctor through to a laboratory/computer facility that can deliver the most accurate information quickly.[42] There are, of course, other technical considerations, such as the economies of scale that may accrue to large centralized units, particularly if they are producing and delivering a standardized benefit.[43]

Among political considerations that influence the organization of social welfare, the degree of public consensus around program benefits carries significant weight. Widespread agreement about the value of benefits and the worthiness of recipients, such as with social security, facilitates centralized arrangements at the federal level. Public disagreement and uncertainty about what benefits should be given and to whom, create political pressures for decentralized structures that will be most responsive to local preferences.

Support for greater decentralization of the American welfare state has been building since the New Federalism, introduced in the early 1970s under the Nixon administration. Promoting the devolution of decision-making authority from the federal to the state level, the New Federalism sought, in Nixon's words, "to set states and localities free—free to set new priorities, free to meet unmet needs, free to make their own mistakes, yes, but also free to score splendid successes which otherwise would never be realized."[44] These objectives were to be accomplished by the provision of federal funds through bloc grants, a method of financing that affords state governments wide discretion in establishing social welfare programs tailored to local needs. Over the last decade these fiscal efforts have shifted increasing responsibility for social welfare policy decisions from federal to state governments. According to national polls, public opinion is highly conducive to movement in this direction based on social perceptions that state government is closer to the people, more sensitive to their needs, and less impersonal than the federal government.[45]

Decentralization is a conventional remedy to the bureaucratic alienation of social welfare functions conducted through large units of central government. Indeed, those who argue for decentralized administration of social welfare under local jurisdiction often conjure up the gemeinschaft vision of communal warmth and solicitude.[46] However, there is another side to localism that is intrusive, parochial, and potentially oppressive. There is also another side to centralized administration. In their lack of concern for personal affairs and special circumstances of social welfare recipients, programs administered by the large bureaucratic apparatus of central government allow greater latitude for privacy and individual freedom.[47]

Beyond the technical constraints and public preferences that enter debates over centralization versus decentralization of social welfare activities, there are two ambiguities in the conceptualization of these alternatives that complicate issues of choice. First, centralized and decentralized administration are relative to both the social systems in which they operate and the levels from which they are perceived in those systems. Thus in dealing with these ideas it is important to be clear about the points of reference. Arrangements that appear decentralized looking down from a higher level may seem extremely centralized from below. The population as well as physical size of different systems also influences perceptions of decentralization. In that regard, comparisons between the organization of the American welfare state and its European counterparts are often deceptive. California, for example, is three times as large as England geographically and has twice the population of Sweden. The devolution of authority from the federal to the state level represents a significant degree of decentralization in the American context. In the operational sense of serving a large population over great distances, however, social welfare administration by state governments in California and other big states is in many ways comparable to what would be considered a highly centralized degree of decision-making authority in England and Sweden.

The second ambiguity concerns the distinction between points at which social welfare benefits are distributed and consumed. Benefits in-kind, such as day care, transportation, legal aid, counseling, and congregate meals are consumed at the point of distribution. Whether centralized or decentralized, the administrative arrangements to provide these benefits pertain simultaneously to distribution and consumption. Cash benefits and vouchers, such as food stamps, are a different case. The distribution of cash benefits, for example, may be centrally administered by the federal government, which has considerable skill and experience in writing checks and assuring their delivery to the appropriate beneficiaries. But the point of consumption is highly decentralized as the locus of decisions about how to use these benefits moves directly into the hands of individual consumers. Thus, focusing on the point of consumption makes it possible to conceive of social welfare programs that provide cash benefits centrally administered at the federal level as representing, in Rivlin's view, the "most extreme form of decentralization."[48]

The final issue in the design of the social market concerns its methods of operation, particularly the degree to which they are influenced by capitalist doctrine. In recent years there has been increasing political pressure for the social market to adopt the modus operandi of the economic market. This trend is agreeable to middle-class recipients who prefer the role of consumer to that of beneficiary; it is also compatible with the interests of welfare professionals oriented toward private practice. As previously suggested, the social market to some extent can accommodate to and benefit from an infusion of competition, choice, profit, self-interest, and other methods and incentives of the market economy. Values inhere in these means as much as in their ends. Employed too vigorously, however, these methods and incentives eventually must vitiate the values and purposes of the social market. Competition and self-interest seldom cultivate equality of material conditions and communal security. The elevation of consumer choice inhibits thoughts of individual sacrifice for the common good. Stringent concerns for economic efficiency lend brief considerations to the adequacy of social provisions. The pursuit of profit engenders little compassion for the economic circumstances of others. In essence, this issue hinges on the contradictory potential of these methods to undermine the broad values of the social market while enhancing the efficiency of its distributive activities. This dualism suggests that neither the total embrace of entrepreneurial methods nor their complete rejection is of maximal advantage to the social market. Between these extremes is another line of action based on careful study that clarifies when, where, and how the social market might adopt specific methods most beneficially. Some initial thoughts along this line were expressed earlier (in chaps. 1 and 2). This middle course aims to selectively adopt entrepreneurial methods without permitting them to distort the social market's purpose or to dominate its essential character as a distributive mechanism responsive to need, dependency, a sense of communal obligation, and charitable sentiments.

PURSUING THE ISSUES: PRAGMATISM REVIVED

The issues identified above form an agenda to delineate the structure and function of the social market in a mixed economy. The suggested approach to these issues adheres to visions of neither capitalist nor socialist Utopias. It follows instead the tenets of pragmatism in quest of a workable balance between the values and objectives of social and economic markets. One might question this approach, arguing that it was pragmatism of the sort that inspired the disjointed and aimless transformation of the American welfare state between the early 1960s and the late 1970s. There is a point to that argument which deserves attention. The pragmatic designs of interest-group liberalism typically focused on social programs, problems, and groups. Lacking synoptic vision of the social market and its relationship to the market economy, the liberal approach generated a vast number of programs intended to solve social problems and to alleviate the needs of various groups. In the absence of a comprehensive perspective on the social market, these programs multiplied with relatively little thought or measurement of their cumulative impact. There was no conceptual map of the welfare state with boundaries, however tentative, beyond which programmatic expansion had to be carefully charted. Thus, the type of liberal pragmatism that induced the proliferation of social welfare programs in the 1960s and 1970s was barely, if at all, influenced by a political philosophy of social balance between welfare and capitalism.

Pragmatism represents a method of knowing that emphasizes continual empirical verification to establish truths which may vary according to time, place, and purpose of inquiry. A prudent inquiry into the ideal balance between social and economic markets requires two developments: elaboration of empirical measurements relating to the scope and functions of the social market, and refinement of the political process through which the truths derived from these measurements are filtered.

The inadequacy of empirical measurements is illustrated by the pressing demand (discussed in chap. 4) for more sensitive indicators of poverty. To achieve political consensus about the proper size and activities of the social market there must be some agreement about the degree of need that is unmet by the economic market. The incidence of poverty is a major criterion of that unmet need. Indeed, the poverty line might be thought of as an empirical referent for the safety net below which members of the community should not be allowed to fall.

There are three practical difficulties in measuring poverty. First is the question of what gets included as income. Under the Social Security Administration's official definition of poverty the level of income for farm families is calculated at 85% that of nonfarm families. This farm differential is based on the estimate that home food production accounts for 31% of the total value of the food consumed by farm families. If in-kind income of this sort is counted on the farm, why not include the value of food stamps and other supplemental food programs such as meals on wheels in calculating nonfarm incomes?[49] Moreover, since food and shelter are major components in a standard of living, would it not be reasonable to count the dollar value of subsidized housing and, perhaps, even home ownership for those who have paid off their mortgages? Once on this path of inquiry it is a short step to push beyond the traditional measure of income and ask that it be combined with a measure of net worth for a more accurate picture of a family's economic circumstances. This revised measure would have a sharp effect on official poverty estimates, as demonstrated by several studies showing that the number of aged poor is reduced by 32 to 35% when the annuitized value of their net worth is added to their cash income.[50]

The second problem involves the technical approach to setting the poverty threshold. There are two perspectives on poverty which entail different types of measurements. From one angle poverty may be viewed in absolute terms that emphasize physical dimensions of deprivation such as lack of nutrition, clothing, and shelter. The Social

Security Administration's definition, for example, is based upon the cost of a subsistence food budget multiplied by a factor of three. The poverty threshold resulting from this formula has been widely criticized.[51] Some critics accept the idea of a nutritional approach but claim that the specific techniques applied in this case underestimate the costs of a minimally adequate standard of living.[52] Others argue that this approach is influenced as much by political constraints and social values as by scientific objectivity.[53]

Poverty is also perceived as a relative phenomenon. This perspective focuses upon social dimensions of deprivation that stem from the difference between how people live and the standard of living they might expect to enjoy in light of community norms. In a fundamental sense poverty is, of course, always relative to time and place. Most people living comfortably by community standards 800 years ago would be considered in a frightful state of poverty today. And even in modern times poor people in the poorest developing countries would view the poverty threshold in most advanced industrial societies as a decent improvement in their circumstances. In the absence of hypothetical illustrations, a problem arises when policymakers try to envision a practical standard against which relative deprivation should be measured.

One yardstick is offered by the renowned poverty analyst Peter Townsend, whose deprivation index attempts to capture the extent to which a family's life-style varies from the customary style of living in the community. The components of Townsend's deprivation index include a family's diet, pattern of recreation, household amenities, and social activities. By correlating the deprivation index scores with household incomes he estimates that 25% of British households are living in poverty, a considerable increase over the 7% rate based on the conventional British definition of poverty at the time of the study.[54] However, like the phenomenon it seeks to interpret, Townsend's index is not without a measure of ambiguity. Variations on several of his life-style indicators may result from cultural differences and individual preferences as much as from the inability to share in the normal standard of living.[55] A diet that excludes fresh meat, for example, is a matter of personal taste for vegetarians.

In the United States proponents of the relative view of poverty favor establishing a poverty threshold at various levels from 35 to 50% of the national median income.[56] These proposals are usually justified by reference to findings from public opinion polls and more detailed social science surveys which report what the citizenry considers the minimum income necessary to make ends meet.[57] In comparison to these proposals, the Social Security Administration's poverty threshold for a family of four has declined from 40.6% of the median income for a family of four in 1965 to 32.8% of their median income in 1979.[58]

Whether viewed from a relative or an absolute perspective there is a third complication in measuring poverty which involves taking account of local variations. The Social Security Administration's definition of poverty virtually ignores the wide range of costs for a subsistence budget based upon local prices across the United States or for that matter even within a state. There are technical complexities, but cost-of-living adjustments can be made with varying degrees of precision.[59] For instance, Canada, with a smaller population that is geographically more concentrated than in the United States, had devised a poverty index that is based on five different cost-of-living estimates related to the population size of a family's area of residence.[60] Estimates for cost-of-living differentials by community size in the United States indicate that the mean amount for a "minimum adequacy" budget in the largest urban areas is about 41% greater than the mean amount in rural areas.[61]

Local variations also confound relative measures of poverty. It is unclear, for example, why the national median income is regularly employed as the appropriate base against which to calculate relative deprivation. This form of deprivation seems to be felt most acutely in relation to the circumstances of one's neighbors—those with whom one interacts on a daily basis. Even beyond the local community, differences among state median incomes, ranging in 1979 from $14,356 to $28,266, are sufficiently large to challenge the intrinsic validity of a national median as the baseline measure for relative deprivation.

While it is possible to construct more refined indicators of poverty, the traditional concept of a poverty line may not be the most useful device for identifying unmet need. As long as a single index of this sort is used to symbolize the demand for a redistribution of resources through the social market it will serve as the focal point for promoting both security and equality. In this position the index would remain at the center of the long-standing struggle to have poverty defined as a level of income inadequate to secure the basic necessities of life versus the interpretation of poverty as inequality. Substituting separate measures explicitly focused upon adequacy of income and relative deprivation for the inclusive index of poverty might permit more lucid discourse on the aims and achievements of the social market.

But to establish practical guidelines for managing the social market involves more than an elaboration of empirical measures of need. There are stores of data that detail the nature of benefits, costs, and beneficiary characteristics for a vast array of social welfare programs. There are also demographic forecasts that anticipate eventual demands for social welfare. Putting these data on unmet needs, current operations, and future claims into a coherent policy framework would assist policymakers in charting a course for the social market based on a synoptic view of the welfare state.

The initial step toward the development of a guidance system for the social market entails the design of an institutional mechanism for gathering, processing, and interpreting information. The Council of Economic Advisers serves such a function in relation to the market economy. There are several bodies, such as the Advisory Council on Public Welfare and the National Advisory Council on Economic Opportunity, that might have provided a similar base of operation for the social market. However, these councils identified more closely with the specific programs they were charged to review and report upon than with a larger vision of the welfare state. In practice they served as interest group advocates for these programs rather than detached professional analysts concerned with balancing competing claims and clarifying alternatives.[62]

The ideal mechanism to oversee the welfare state would be a public body, perhaps an "Advisory Council on Social Welfare," instructed to examine the data, to plot the tentative boundaries of the social market, and to explore the values and present the facts that inform choices about the future course of events. The membership would be drawn from several disciplines to encourage the organization and interpretation of facts in light of social, political, and economic considerations. Annual reports issued by this body would identify trends in benefit allocations, forecast impending claims, and illuminate the central issues that call for continual adjustments in the scope and functions of the social market. A guidance mechanism of this sort might elevate the level of political debate, investing it with a degree of precision and tempering it with a quality of moderation that distinguish neither the liberal allies, who animated the welfare state through the late 1970s, nor the conservative opposition, which has come to power in the early 1980s.

The search for a workable balance between the economic and social markets of a mixed economy poses a crucial challenge to the future of the welfare state in a capitalist society. It is a challenge that demands sober regard for both the vitality of private enterprise and the humanity of social welfare.

NOTES

1. For example, see Frances Piven and Richard Cloward, *Regulating the Poor* (New York: Random House, 1971).

2. For example, see Milton Friedman and Rose Friedman, *Free to Choose* (New York: Avon, 1979).

3. T. B. Bottomore and Maximilien Rubel, eds., *Karl Marx: Selected Writings in Sociology and Social Philosophy*, trans. T. B. Bottomore (New York: McGraw-Hill, 1964), p. 258.

4. This approach is suggested by Ian Gough, *The Political Economy of the Welfare State* (London: Macmillan, 1979).

5. See Gabriel Kolko, *Wealth and Power in America* (New York: Praeger, 1962), and Robert Morris, *Social Policy of the American Welfare State* (New York: Harper & Row, 1979), pp. 62–63.

6. U.S. Bureau of the Census, *Statistical Abstract of the United States: 1981* (Washington, D.C.: U.S. GPO, 1981), p. 438.

7. Irving Kristol, *Two Cheers for Capitalism* (New York: Mentor, 1978), p. 185.

8. U.S. Department of Housing and Urban Development, *How Well Are We Housed? Volume 4: The Elderly* (Washington D.C.: U.S. GPO, 1979).

9. Thomas Sowell, "Thoughts and Details on Poverty," *Policy Review*, 17 (Summer 1981), 16.

10. Morton Paglin, "The Measurement and Trend of Inequality: A Basic Revision," *American Economic Review*, 65 (Sept. 1975), 598–609. According to the standard measure of inequality, the lowest quintile in 1972 received only 5.4% of the national income, which was 27% (5.4/20) of the income share that theoretically would accrue to them under conditions of perfect equality. Paglin's analysis shows that, after controlling for the age distribution of income recipients, the bottom fifth received 41.9% of the income that would accrue to them in a perfectly egalitarian society.

11. Asa Briggs, "The Welfare State in Historical Perspective," *Social Welfare Institutions*, ed. Mayer Zald (New York: Wiley & Sons, 1965), p. 62.

12. Bottomore and Rubel, *Marx*, p. 246. For a critical discussion of Marx's materialistic interpretation of history see H. B. Mayo, *Democracy and Marxism* (New York: Oxford University Press, 1955), pp. 38–66, and Karl Popper, *The Open Society and Its Enemies* (Princeton: Princeton University Press, 1950), pp. 292–301.

13. Richard Hofstadter, *Social Darwinism in American Thought*, rev. ed. (Boston: Beacon Press, 1962), pp. 200–04.

14. Lionel Robbins, "The Economic Functions of the State in English Classical Political Economy," *Private Wants and Public Needs*, ed. Edmund Phelps (New York: Norton, 1965), pp. 96–103.

15. Milton Friedman, *Capitalism and Freedom* (Chicago: University of Chicago Press, 1962), p. 191.

16. Friedrich Hayek, *The Road to Serfdom* (Chicago: University of Chicago Press, 1944), p. 120.

17. For an analysis of the assumptions and inconsistencies of classical capitalism's tolerance of the welfare state see Robert Sugden, "Hard Luck Stories: The Problem of the Uninsured in a Laissez-Faire Society," *Journal of Social Policy*, 11 (Apr. 1982), 201–16.

18. Friedman, *Capitalism and Freedom*. Also see Friedman and Friedman, *Free to Choose*, pp. 110–15.

19. Hayek, *Road to Serfdom*, pp. 32–42.

20. This school of thought, which includes guild socialists, Owenists, and others supporting various forms of industrial democracy and localism, is sometimes referred to generically as "communitarian socialism." For a discussion of the communitarian viewpoint see Erich Fromm, *The Sane Society* (New York: Holt, Rinehart and Winston, 1955), pp. 283–86.

21. Harry Specht, "The Grass Roots and Government in Social Planning and Community Organization," *Administration in Social Work*, 2 (Fall 1978), 319–34. Also see Neil Gilbert, "The Design of Community Planning Structures," *Social Service Review*, 53 (Dec. 1979), 646–47.

22. Roger Hadley and Stephen Hatch, *Social Welfare and the Failure of the State* (London: Allen & Unwin, 1981), p. 111.

23. Mary Murphy, "The Role of the Fabian Society in British Affairs," *British Socialism Today*, ed. Julia Johnsen (New York: H. W. Wilson, 1950), pp. 17–23.

24. As Mishra points out, this wider view of social welfare draws close to the Marxist perspective (Ramesh Mishra, *Society and Social Policy* [London: Macmillan, 1977], pp. 88–89).

25. Richard Titmuss, *Essays on 'The Welfare State'* (London: Unwin University Books, 1958), pp. 34–55.

26. Marc Landy and Henry Plotkin, "Limits of the Market Metaphor," *Transaction/Society*, 19 (May/June 1982), 8–17.

27. Robert Pinker, *The Idea of Welfare* (London: Heinemann, 1979), p. 252.

28. For example, see D. A. Reisman, *Richard Titmuss: Welfare and Society* (London: Heinemann, 1977), pp. 68–79; Gaston Rimlinger, *Welfare Policy and Industrialization in Europe, America and Russia* (New York: Wiley & Sons, 1971), pp. 335–43; and Morris Janowitz, *Social Control of the Welfare State* (New York: Elsevier, 1976).

29. See James O'Connor, *The Fiscal Crisis of the State* (New York: St. Martin's Press, 1973), and Piven and Cloward, *Regulating the Poor.*

30. Rein suggests that the study of social purposes constitutes the central puzzle of social policy (Martin Rein, *Social Policy: Issues of Choice and Change* [New York: Random House, 1970], p. 9).

31. Titmuss, *Essays.*

32. Robert Pear, "Reagan Weighs Health Premium Tax," *New York Times,* Jan. 11, 1983, p. 7.

33. For a more detailed analysis of various sides of this issue see Harold Wilensky and Charles Lebeaux, *Industrial Society and Social Welfare* (New York: Russell Sage, 1958), pp. 140–47.

34. Mishra, *Society and Social Policy,* p. 107.

35. Kristol, *Two Cheers for Capitalism,* p. 194.

36. T. H. Marshall, *The Right to Welfare and Other Essays* (London: Heinemann, 1981), p. 133.

37. Ibid., p. 134.

38. Gavyn Davies and David Piachaud, "Social Policy and the Economy," in *The Future of the Welfare State,* ed. Howard Glennerster (London: Heinemann, 1983), Table 4.3, p. 47.

39. Friedman, *Capitalism and Freedom,* pp. 23–36.

40. Marshall, *Right to Welfare,* p. 133.

41. Daniel P. Moynihan, "Comments on 'Restructuring the Government of New York City,'" in *The Neighborhoods, The City and The Region: Working Papers on Jurisdiction and Structure,* State Study Commission for New York City, Jan. 1973, p. 15.

42. Ibid., p. 16.

43. Many of the personal social services that deal with therapy, counseling, and advice employ an intensive form of technology under which the treatment plan varies in light of constant feedback concerning the state of the client. Customed to individual cases, these types of service are less likely to benefit from the economies of large-scale organization than services which deliver a highly standardized provision, such as food and clothing. See Neil Gilbert and Harry Specht, *Dimensions of Social Welfare Policy* (Englewood Cliffs: Prentice-Hall, 1974), p. 85.

44. Richard Nixon, "Message to Congress on General Revenue Sharing" (Feb. 4, 1971), in *Weekly Compilation of Presidential Documents,* 7 (Feb. 8, 1971), p. 170.

45. Martin Anderson, *Welfare: The Political Economy of Welfare Reform* (Palo Alto: Hoover Institution Press, 1981), p. 165.

46. See, for example, the proposals by Paul Goodman, *Utopian Essays and Practical Proposals* (New York: Vintage, 1964), pp. 12–13.

47. For discussion of these aspects of decentralization see Grant McConnell, *Private Power and American Democracy* (New York: Knopf, 1966), p. 107.

48. Alice Rivlin, *Systematic Thinking for Social Action* (Washington, D.C.: Brookings Institution, 1971), p. 122.

49. For discussion of this issue see Thomas Carlin, Linda Ghelfi, and Janet Coffin, "The Farm Differential in the Poverty Threshold: Should It Be Changed?" in *Aspects of Welfare and Poverty in Rural America: Two Issue Briefs,* Economic Development

Division, Economics, Statistics and Cooperative Services, U.S. Dept. of Agriculture, Washington, D.C., Nov. 1979, pp. 11–18.

50. The 32% reduction is based on net worth annuitized at a 10% rate as calculated by Burton Weisbrod and W. Lee Hansen, "An Income-Net Worth Approach to Measuring Economic Welfare," *American Economic Review*, 8 (Dec. 1968), 1315–29. The 35% rate is reported in J. Murray, "Potential Income from Assets: Findings of the 1963 Survey of the Aged," *Social Security Bulletin*, 24 (Dec. 1964), 3–11.

51. See, for example, Mollie Orshansky et al., "Measuring Poverty: A Debate," *Public Welfare*, 33 (Spring 1975), 46–55; Donald Chambers, "Another Look at Poverty Lines in England and the United States," *Social Service Review*, 55 (Sept. 1981), 472–83; and S. M. Miller and Pamela Roby, *The Future of Inequality* (New York: Basic Books, 1970), pp. 23–29.

52. Arthur Blaustein, ed., *The American Promise: Equal Justice and Economic Opportunity* (New Brunswick, N.J.: Transaction Books, 1982), p. 52.

53. Rein, *Social Policy*, pp. 446–60.

54. Peter Townsend, *Poverty in the United Kingdom: A Survey of Household Resources and Standards of Living* (Berkeley: University of California Press, 1979).

55. For an incisive critique of Townsend's index see David Piachaud, "Peter Townsend and the Holy Grail," *New Society*, 57: 982 (Sept. 10, 1981), 419–21.

56. Kenneth Keniston and the Carnegie Council on Children, *All Our Children* (New York: Harcourt Brace Jovanovich, 1977), pp. 26–31; Miller and Roby, *Future of Inequality*.; Dean A. Worcester, Jr., "Blueprint for a Welfare State That Contributes to Economic Efficiency," *Social Service Review*, 54 (June 1980), 177–78.

57. Lee Rainwater, *What Money Buys* (New York: Basic Books, 1976); Theo Geodhart et al., "The Poverty Line: Concept and Measurement," *Journal of Human Resources*, 12 (Fall 1977), 503–20.

58. U.S. Bureau of the Census, *Statistical Abstract of the United States: 1981* (Washington, D.C.: U.S. GPO, 1981), p. 446.

59. The farm differential is not an adjustment for the costs of living in rural areas. Rather it takes account of food produced at home.

60. J. R. Podoluk, *Incomes of Canadians* (Ottawa: Queen's Printer, 1968).

61. Rainwater, *What Money Buys*, p. 57.

62. The National Advisory Council on Economic Opportunity was abolished by the Reagan administration in 1981. Its final report is a strident polemic indicting the social policies of the 1980s. See Blaustein, *American Promise*.

INDEX

21